HERSHEY'S®

Incredibly Easy
Recipes

Publications International, Ltd.

Front and back cover photography and photography on pages 17, 29, 39, 61, 65, 67, 89, 93, 97, 103, 121, 123, 131, 147, and 151 by Stephen Hamilton Photographics, Inc, Chicago.

Photographers: Raymond Barrera, Jennifer Marx
Photographers' Assistants: Matt Savage, Jason McDonald
Prop Stylist: Andrea Kuhn
Food Stylists: Kathy Joy, Walter Moeller
Assistant Food Stylists: Elaine Funk, Jill Kaczanowski

Pictured on front cover: Brownie Cheesecake (*page 68*).

Pictured on back cover: Rocky Road Tasty Team Treats (*page 60*).

ISBN-13: 978-1-4127-9938-6
ISBN-10: 1-4127-9938-4

Library of Congress Control Number: 2008920412

Manufactured in China.

8 7 6 5 4 3 2 1

Microwave Cooking: Microwave ovens vary in wattage. Use the cooking times as guidelines and check for doneness before adding more time.

CONTENTS

COOKIES

Rich Dark Tiger Cookies

Makes about 4 dozen cookies

1¹/₂ **cups granulated sugar**

¹/₂ **cup vegetable oil**

¹/₂ **cup HERSHEY'S SPECIAL DARK Cocoa or HERSHEY'S Cocoa**

3 **eggs**

1¹/₂ **teaspoons vanilla extract**

1³/₄ **cups all-purpose flour**

1¹/₂ **teaspoons baking powder**

¹/₂ **teaspoon salt**

Powdered sugar

48 **HERSHEY'S KISSES** BRAND **SPECIAL DARK Chocolates or HERSHEY'S KISSES** BRAND **Milk Chocolates, unwrapped (optional)**

1. Stir together granulated sugar and oil in large bowl; add cocoa, beating until well blended. Beat in eggs and vanilla. Stir together flour, baking powder and salt; gradually add to cocoa mixture, beating well.

2. Cover; refrigerate until dough is firm enough to handle, at least 6 hours.

3. Heat oven to 350°F. Grease cookie sheet or line with parchment paper. Shape dough into 1-inch balls (dough will still be sticky); roll in powdered sugar to coat. Place about 2 inches apart on prepared cookie sheet.

4. Bake 11 to 13 minutes or until almost no indentation remains when touched lightly and tops are cracked. Immediately press chocolate piece into center of each cookie, if desired. Cool slightly. Transfer to wire rack. Cool completely.

HERSHEY'S SPECIAL DARK Chips and Macadamia Nut Cookies

Makes 3^1/$_2$ dozen cookies

6 tablespoons butter, softened

^{1}/$_3$ cup butter flavored shortening

^{1}/$_2$ cup packed light brown sugar

^{1}/$_3$ cup granulated sugar

1 egg

1^1/$_2$ teaspoons vanilla extract

1^1/$_3$ cups all-purpose flour

^{1}/$_2$ teaspoon baking soda

^{1}/$_2$ teaspoon salt

2 cups (12-ounce package) HERSHEY'S SPECIAL DARK Chocolate Chips

^{1}/$_2$ cup MAUNA LOA Macadamia Nut Baking Pieces

1. Heat oven to 350°F.

2. Beat butter and shortening in large bowl until well blended. Add brown sugar and granulated sugar; beat thoroughly. Add egg and vanilla, beating until well blended. Stir together flour, baking soda and salt; gradually beat into butter mixture. Stir in chocolate chips and nuts. Drop by rounded teaspoons onto ungreased cookie sheet.

3. Bake 10 to 12 minutes or until edges are lightly browned. Cool slightly; transfer to wire rack. Cool completely.

White Chips and Macadamia Pieces Variation: Substitute 2 cups (12-ounce package) HERSHEY'S Premier White Chips for HERSHEY'S SPECIAL DARK Chocolate Chips. Prepare as directed above.

Chocolate Cookie Variation: Decrease flour to 1 cup; add ^{1}/$_3$ cup HERSHEY'S Cocoa or HERSHEY'S SPECIAL DARK Cocoa.

Peanut Butter Blossoms

Makes 4 dozen cookies

48 **HERSHEY'S KISSES** BRAND **Milk Chocolates**

3/4 **cup REESE'S Creamy Peanut Butter**

1/2 **cup shortening**

1/3 **cup granulated sugar**

1/3 **cup packed light brown sugar**

1 **egg**

2 **tablespoons milk**

1 **teaspoon vanilla extract**

1 1/2 **cups all-purpose flour**

1 **teaspoon baking soda**

1/2 **teaspoon salt**

Granulated sugar

1. Heat oven to 375°F. Remove wrappers from chocolates.

2. Beat peanut butter and shortening with electric mixer on medium speed in large bowl until well blended. Add 1/3 cup granulated sugar and brown sugar; beat until fluffy. Add egg, milk and vanilla; beat well. Stir together flour, baking soda and salt; gradually beat into peanut butter mixture.

3. Shape dough into 1-inch balls. Roll in additional granulated sugar; place on ungreased cookie sheet.

4. Bake 8 to 10 minutes or until lightly browned. Immediately press a chocolate into center of each cookie; cookies will crack around edges. Remove to wire racks and cool completely.

Peanut Butter Cut-Out Cookies
Makes about 3 dozen cookies

$^1/_2$ **cup (1 stick) butter or margarine**

1 **cup REESE'S Peanut Butter Chips**

$^2/_3$ **cup packed light brown sugar**

1 **egg**

$^3/_4$ **teaspoon vanilla extract**

$1^1/_3$ **cups all-purpose flour**

$^3/_4$ **teaspoon baking soda**

$^1/_2$ **cup finely chopped pecans**

CHOCOLATE CHIP GLAZE (recipe follows)

1. Place butter and peanut butter chips in medium saucepan; cook over low heat, stirring constantly, until melted. Pour into large bowl; add brown sugar, egg and vanilla, beating until well blended. Stir in flour, baking soda and pecans, blending well. Refrigerate 15 to 20 minutes or until firm enough to roll.

2. Heat oven to 350°F.

3. Roll a small portion of dough at a time on lightly floured board, or between 2 pieces of wax paper, to $^1/_4$-inch thickness. (Keep remaining dough in refrigerator.) With cookie cutters, cut dough into desired shapes; place on ungreased cookie sheets.

4. Bake 7 to 8 minutes or until almost set (do not overbake). Cool 1 minute; remove from cookie sheets to wire racks. Cool completely. Drizzle CHOCOLATE CHIP GLAZE onto each cookie; allow to set.

CHOCOLATE CHIP GLAZE: Place 1 cup HERSHEY'S SPECIAL DARK Chocolate Chips or HERSHEY'S Semi-Sweet Chocolate Chips and 1 tablespoon shortening (do not use butter, margarine spread or oil) in small microwave-safe bowl. Microwave at MEDIUM (50%) 1 minute; stir. If necessary, microwave at MEDIUM an additional 15 seconds at a time, stirring after each heating, just until chips are melted and mixture is smooth.

Classic MINI KISSES Cookie Mix (Cookie Mix in a Jar)

Makes 1 quart (4 cups) mix

2¼ cups all-purpose flour

⅔ cup granulated sugar

1 teaspoon baking soda

½ teaspoon salt

1½ cups HERSHEY'S MINI KISSES BRAND Milk Chocolates, divided

⅔ cup packed light brown sugar

BAKING INSTRUCTIONS (recipe follows)

1. Stir together flour, granulated sugar, baking soda and salt. Transfer mixture to clean 1-quart (4-cup) glass jar with lid; pack down into bottom of jar.

2. Layer with 1 cup HERSHEY'S MINI KISSES BRAND Milk Chocolates and brown sugar.* Top with remaining ½ cup chocolates; close jar. Attach card with BAKING INSTRUCTIONS.

To increase shelf life of mix, wrap brown sugar in plastic wrap and press into place.

Classic MINI KISSES Cookies

Makes 36 cookies

1 jar Classic MINI KISSES BRAND Cookies Mix

1 cup (2 sticks) butter, softened and cut into pieces

1 teaspoon vanilla extract

2 eggs, lightly beaten

1. Heat oven to 375°F.

2. Spoon contents of jar into large bowl; stir to break up any lumps. Add butter and vanilla; stir until crumbly mixture forms. Add eggs; stir to form smooth, very stiff dough. Drop by heaping teaspoons onto ungreased cookie sheet.

3. Bake 8 to 10 minutes or until lightly browned. Cool slightly; remove from cookie sheet to wire rack. Cool completely.

Lemon Coconut Pixies

Makes about 4 dozen cookies

$^1/_4$ **cup ($^1/_2$ stick) butter or margarine, softened**

1 **cup granulated sugar**

2 **eggs**

$1^1/_2$ **teaspoons freshly grated lemon peel**

$1^1/_2$ **cups all-purpose flour**

2 **teaspoons baking powder**

$^1/_4$ **teaspoon salt**

1 **cup MOUNDS Sweetened Coconut Flakes**

Powdered sugar

1. Heat oven to 300°F.

2. Beat butter, granulated sugar, eggs and lemon peel in large bowl until well blended. Stir together flour, baking powder and salt; gradually add to lemon mixture, beating until blended. Stir in coconut. Cover; refrigerate dough about 1 hour or until firm enough to handle. Shape into 1-inch balls; roll in powdered sugar. Place 2 inches apart on ungreased cookie sheet.

3. Bake 15 to 18 minutes or until edges are set. Immediately remove from cookie sheet to wire rack. Cool completely. Store in tightly covered container in cool, dry place.

KISSES Macaroon Cookies

Makes about 4 dozen cookies

1/3 **cup butter or margarine, softened**

1 **package (3 ounces) cream cheese, softened**

3/4 **cup sugar**

1 **egg yolk**

2 **teaspoons almond extract**

2 **teaspoons orange juice**

1¼ **cups all-purpose flour**

2 **teaspoons baking powder**

1/4 **teaspoon salt**

5 **cups MOUNDS Sweetened Coconut Flakes, divided**

48 **HERSHEY'S KISSES** BRAND **Milk Chocolates**

1. Beat butter, cream cheese and sugar with electric mixer on medium speed in large bowl until well blended. Add egg yolk, almond extract and orange juice; beat well. Stir together flour, baking powder and salt; gradually add to butter mixture. Stir in 3 cups coconut. Cover; refrigerate 1 hour or until firm enough to handle. Meanwhile, remove wrappers from chocolates.

2. Heat oven to 350°F.

3. Shape dough into 1-inch balls; roll in remaining 2 cups coconut. Place on ungreased cookie sheet.

4. Bake 10 to 12 minutes or until lightly browned. Immediately press chocolate piece into center of each cookie. Cool 1 minute. Carefully remove to wire rack and cool completely.

Peanut Butter Fun Filled Cookies

Makes 30 cookies

$1/2$ **cup (1 stick) butter or margarine, softened**

$3/4$ **cup sugar**

$1/3$ **cup REESE'S Creamy Peanut Butter**

1 **egg**

$1/2$ **teaspoon vanilla extract**

$1\,1/4$ **cups all-purpose flour**

$1/2$ **teaspoon baking soda**

$1/4$ **teaspoon salt**

$1\,1/3$ **cups (8-ounce package) REESE'S Milk Chocolate Baking Pieces Filled with Peanut Butter Crème**

1. Heat oven to 350°F.

2. Beat butter, sugar and peanut butter in large bowl until creamy. Add egg and vanilla; beat well. Stir together flour, baking soda and salt; add to butter mixture, blending well. Stir in baking pieces. Drop by heaping teaspoons onto ungreased cookie sheet.

3. Bake 12 to 14 minutes or until light golden brown around the edges. Cool 1 minute; remove from cookie sheet to wire rack. Cool completely.

White Chip Apricot Oatmeal Cookies

Makes about 3^1/$_2$ dozen cookies

3/4 cup (1^1/$_2$ sticks) butter or margarine, softened

^{1}/$_2$ cup granulated sugar

^{1}/$_2$ cup packed light brown sugar

2 eggs

1 cup all-purpose flour

1 teaspoon baking soda

2^1/$_2$ cups rolled oats

2 cups (12-ounce package) HERSHEY'S Premier White Chips

1 cup chopped dried apricots

1. Heat oven to 375°F.

2. Beat butter, granulated sugar and brown sugar in large bowl until fluffy. Add eggs; beat well. Add flour and baking soda; beat until well blended. Stir in oats, white chips and apricots. Loosely form rounded teaspoon dough into balls; place on ungreased cookie sheet.

3. Bake 7 to 9 minutes or just until lightly browned. Do not overbake. Cool 1 to 2 minutes; remove from cookie sheet to wire rack. Cool completely.

Almond Mini Chip Shortbread

Makes about 3 dozen bars

1 cup (2 sticks) butter (no substitutes), softened

^{1}/$_2$ cup sugar

2^1/$_2$ cups all-purpose flour

1 teaspoon almond extract

1 cup HERSHEY'S Mini Chips Semi-Sweet Chocolate

1. Heat oven to 350°F. Grease 13×9×2-inch baking pan.

2. Beat butter and sugar in large bowl until fluffy. Add flour and almond extract; blend well. Stir in small chocolate chips; pat into prepared pan.

3. Bake 30 minutes or until golden brown. Cool 10 minutes; cut into bars. Cool completely in pan on wire rack.

White Chip Apricot
Oatmeal Cookies

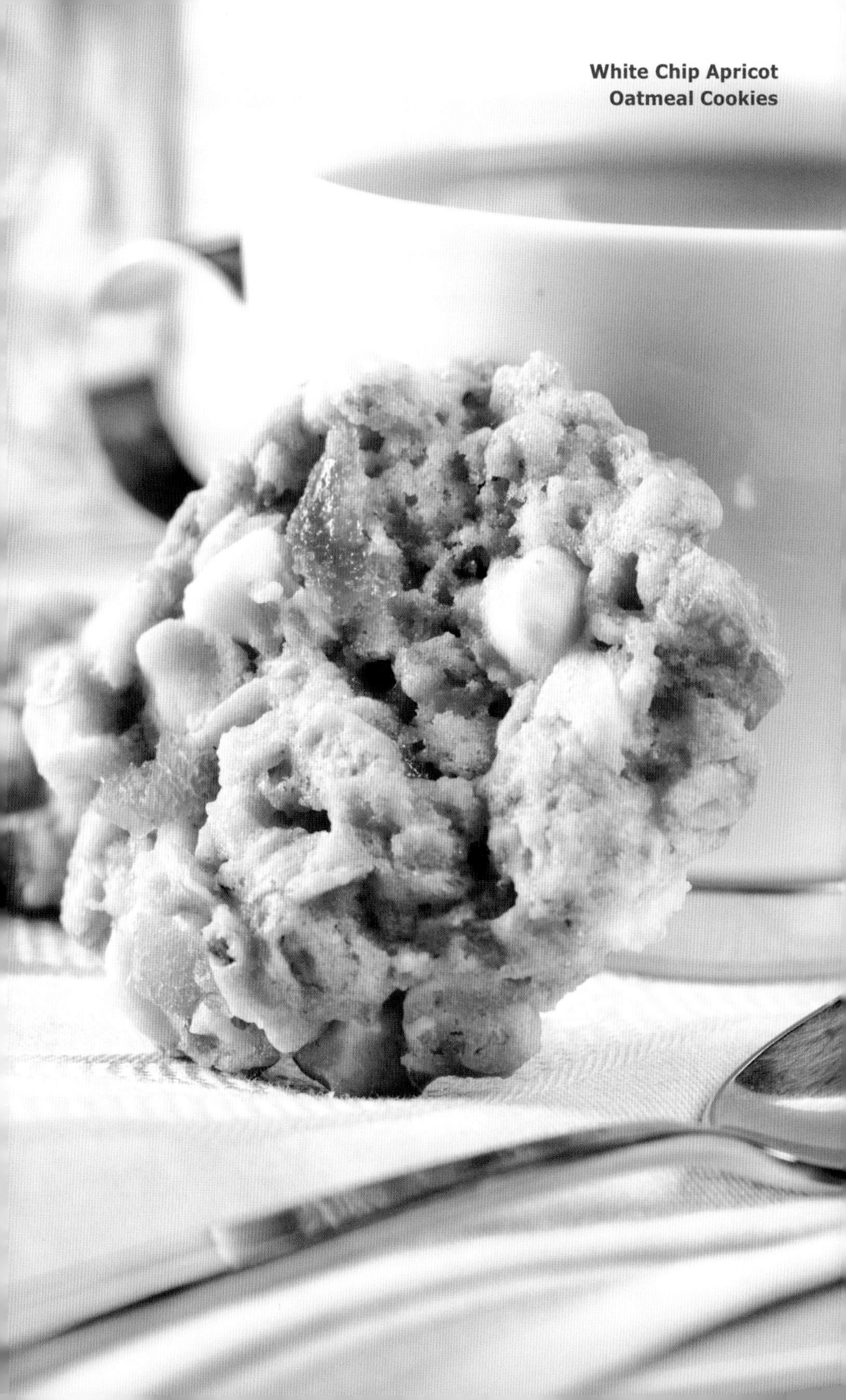

Fudgey Coconut Clusters

Makes about 2^1/$_2$ dozen cookies

5^1/$_3$ cups **MOUNDS Sweetened Coconut Flakes**

1 can (14 ounces) **sweetened condensed milk (not evaporated milk)**

^{2}/$_3$ cup **HERSHEY'S Cocoa**

^{1}/$_4$ cup (^{1}/$_2$ stick) butter or **margarine, melted**

2 teaspoons **vanilla extract**

1^1/$_2$ teaspoons **almond extract**

HERSHEY'S MINI KISSES BRAND **Milk Chocolates or candied cherry halves (optional)**

1. Heat oven to 350°F. Line cookie sheets with aluminum foil; generously grease foil with vegetable shortening.

2. Combine coconut, sweetened condensed milk, cocoa, melted butter, vanilla and almond extract in large bowl; mix well. Drop by rounded tablespoons onto prepared cookie sheets.

3. Bake 9 to 11 minutes or just until set; press 3 milk chocolates or candied cherry halves in center of each cookie, if desired. Immediately remove cookies to wire racks and cool completely.

Chocolate Chip Macaroons: Omit melted butter and cocoa; stir together other ingredients. Add 1 cup HERSHEY'S Mini Chips Semi-Sweet Chocolate. Bake 9 to 11 minutes or just until set. Immediately remove to wire racks and cool completely.

22

Oatmeal Butterscotch Cookies

Makes about 4 dozen cookies

3/4 cup (1 1/2 sticks) butter or margarine, softened

3/4 cup granulated sugar

3/4 cup packed light brown sugar

2 eggs

1 teaspoon vanilla extract

1 1/4 cups all-purpose flour

1 teaspoon baking soda

1/2 teaspoon salt

1/2 teaspoon ground cinnamon

3 cups quick-cooking or regular rolled oats, uncooked

1 3/4 cups (11-ounce package) HERSHEY'S Butterscotch Chips

1. Heat oven to 375°F.

2. Beat butter, granulated sugar and brown sugar in large bowl with electric mixer on medium speed until well blended. Add eggs and vanilla; blend thoroughly. Stir together flour, baking soda, salt and cinnamon; gradually add to butter mixture, beating until well blended. Stir in oats and butterscotch chips; mix well. Drop by teaspoons onto ungreased cookie sheet.

3. Bake 8 to 10 minutes or until golden brown. Cool slightly on pan. Remove to wire rack and cool completely.

Grandma's Favorite Sugarcakes

Makes 3 dozen cookies

2/3 cup butter or margarine, softened

1 1/2 cups packed light brown sugar

1 cup granulated sugar

2 eggs

2 teaspoons vanilla extract

4 1/2 cups all-purpose flour

2 teaspoons baking soda

1 teaspoon baking powder

1 teaspoon salt

1 cup buttermilk or sour milk*

2 cups (12-ounce package) HERSHEY'S Mini Chips Semi-Sweet Chocolate

2 cups chopped walnuts or pecans

Vanilla frosting (optional)

Colored sugar or sprinkles (optional)

To sour milk: Use 1 tablespoon white vinegar plus milk to equal 1 cup.

1. Heat oven to 350°F. Grease cookie sheet.

2. Beat butter, brown sugar and granulated sugar until well blended in large mixing bowl. Add eggs and vanilla; beat until creamy. Stir together flour, baking soda, baking powder and salt; add alternately with buttermilk to butter mixture, beating well after each addition. Stir in small chocolate chips and nuts. Drop by level 1/4 cups or heaping tablespoons 2 inches apart onto prepared cookie sheet.

3. Bake 12 to 14 minutes or until golden brown. Remove to wire rack and cool completely. Frost with favorite vanilla frosting; garnish with colored sugar, if desired.

Chocolate Chip & Toffee Bits Cookies

Makes about 4 dozen cookies

$2^1/_4$ **cups all-purpose flour**

1 **teaspoon baking soda**

$^1/_2$ **teaspoon salt**

$^3/_4$ **cup ($1^1/_2$ sticks) butter or margarine, softened**

$^3/_4$ **cup granulated sugar**

$^3/_4$ **cup packed light brown sugar**

1 **teaspoon vanilla extract**

2 **eggs**

1 **cup HEATH BITS 'O BRICKLE Toffee Bits**

1 **cup HERSHEY'S SPECIAL DARK Chocolate Chips or HERSHEY'S Semi-Sweet Chocolate Chips**

1. Heat oven to 375°F.

2. Stir together flour, baking soda and salt in medium bowl. Beat butter, granulated sugar, brown sugar and vanilla in large bowl until well blended. Add eggs; beat well. Gradually add flour mixture, beating well. Stir in toffee bits and chocolate chips. Drop dough by rounded teaspoons onto ungreased cookie sheet.

3. Bake 8 to 10 minutes or until lightly browned. Cool slightly; remove from cookie sheet to wire rack. Cool completely.

Toffee Studded Snickerdoodles

Makes about 5 dozen cookies

¹/₂ **cup (1 stick) butter or margarine, softened**

¹/₂ **cup shortening**

1 **cup plus 3 tablespoons sugar, divided**

2 **eggs**

2³/₄ **cups all-purpose flour**

2 **teaspoons cream of tartar**

1 **teaspoon baking soda**

¹/₄ **teaspoon salt**

1¹/₃ **cups (8-ounce package) HEATH BITS 'O BRICKLE Toffee Bits**

1 **teaspoon ground cinnamon**

1. Heat oven to 400°F.

2. Beat butter, shortening and 1 cup sugar in large bowl until fluffy. Add eggs; beat thoroughly. Stir together flour, cream of tartar, baking soda and salt; gradually add to butter mixture, beating until well blended. Stir in toffee bits.

3. Stir together remaining 3 tablespoons sugar and cinnamon. Shape dough into 1¹/₄-inch balls; roll in sugar-cinnamon mixture. Place on ungreased cookie sheets.

4. Bake 9 to 11 minutes or until lightly browned around edges. Cool 1 minute; remove from cookie sheets to wire racks. Cool completely.

Cinnamon Chip Apple Cookies

Makes about 4 dozen cookies

3/4 cup (1 1/2 sticks) butter or margarine, softened

1 cup packed light brown sugar

1 egg

1 tablespoon apple juice or water

1/2 teaspoon vanilla extract

1 1/2 cups all-purpose flour

1 teaspoon baking powder

1/2 teaspoon baking soda

1/4 teaspoon salt

1 1/2 cups quick-cooking oats

1 2/3 cups (10-ounce package) HERSHEY'S Cinnamon Chips

1 cup chopped, peeled apple

1/2 cup raisins

1. Heat oven to 350°F. Lightly grease cookie sheet.

2. Beat butter, brown sugar, egg, apple juice and vanilla in large bowl until creamy. Stir together flour, baking powder, baking soda and salt. Add to butter mixture; beat until blended. Stir in oats. Add cinnamon chips, apple and raisins; stir until blended. Drop by teaspoons onto prepared cookie sheet.

3. Bake 10 minutes or until edges are lightly browned. Cool 1 minute; remove from cookie sheet to wire rack. Cool completely.

Chewy Chocolate Oatmeal Cookies

Makes 4 to 5 dozen cookies

1/2 **cup (1 stick) butter or margarine, melted**

1/2 **cup HERSHEY'S Cocoa**

1 **can (14 ounces) sweetened condensed milk (not evaporated milk)**

2 **eggs, beaten**

2 **teaspoons vanilla extract**

1 1/2 **cups quick-cooking rolled oats**

1 **cup all-purpose biscuit baking mix**

1/4 **teaspoon salt**

2 **cups (12-ounce package) HERSHEY'S Premier White Chips**

1 2/3 **cups (10-ounce package) REESE'S Peanut Butter Chips**

1. Heat oven to 350°F. Lightly grease cookie sheet.

2. Stir together butter and cocoa in large bowl until mixture is smooth. Stir in sweetened condensed milk, eggs, vanilla extract, oats, baking mix, salt, white chips and peanut butter chips until well blended. Let batter rest 10 minutes; drop by heaping teaspoons onto prepared cookie sheet.

3. Bake 7 to 9 minutes or until cookies are set and tops begin to dry (do not overbake). Cool 5 minutes; remove from cookie sheet to wire rack. Cool completely. Store in airtight container.

Variation: Omit 1 2/3 cups (10-ounce package) chips; use only 1 package of desired flavor chips.

33

BARS & BROWNIES

Chocolate-Almond Honeys

Makes 20 bars

1³/₄ **cups graham cracker crumbs**

1 **can (14 ounces) sweetened condensed milk (not evaporated milk)**

2 **tablespoons honey**

2 **tablespoons orange or apple juice**

1 **teaspoon freshly grated orange peel**

1 **cup HERSHEY'S SPECIAL DARK Chocolate Chips or HERSHEY'S Semi-Sweet Chocolate Chips**

¹/₂ **cup chopped blanched almonds**

1. Heat oven to 350°F. Grease 9-inch square baking pan.

2. Stir together graham cracker crumbs, sweetened condensed milk, honey, orange juice and orange peel in large bowl. Stir in chocolate chips and almonds. Spread batter in prepared pan.

3. Bake 30 minutes or until golden brown. Cool completely in pan on wire rack. Cut into bars.

Rocky Road Brownies

Makes about 20 brownies

$1^{1}/_{4}$ **cups miniature marshmallows**

1 **cup HERSHEY'S SPECIAL DARK Chocolate Chips or HERSHEY'S Semi-Sweet Chocolate Chips**

$^{1}/_{2}$ **cup chopped nuts**

$^{1}/_{2}$ **cup (1 stick) butter or margarine**

1 **cup sugar**

2 **eggs**

1 **teaspoon vanilla extract**

$^{1}/_{2}$ **cup all-purpose flour**

$^{1}/_{3}$ **cup HERSHEY'S Cocoa**

$^{1}/_{2}$ **teaspoon baking powder**

$^{1}/_{2}$ **teaspoon salt**

1. Heat oven to 350°F. Grease 9-inch square baking pan.

2. Stir together marshmallows, chocolate chips and nuts; set aside. Place butter in large microwave-safe bowl. Microwave at MEDIUM (50%) 1 to $1^{1}/_{2}$ minutes or until melted. Add sugar, eggs and vanilla, beating with spoon until well blended. Add flour, cocoa, baking powder and salt; blend well. Spread batter in prepared pan.

3. Bake 22 minutes. Sprinkle chocolate chip mixture over top. Continue baking 5 minutes or until marshmallows have softened and puffed slightly. Cool completely. With wet knife, cut into squares.

All American HEATH Brownies

Makes 12 brownies

^{1}/$_3$ cup butter or margarine

3 sections (^{1}/$_2$ ounce each) HERSHEY'S Unsweetened Chocolate Premium Baking Bar

1 cup sugar

2 eggs

1 teaspoon vanilla extract

1 cup all-purpose flour

^{1}/$_2$ teaspoon baking powder

^{1}/$_4$ teaspoon salt

1^1/$_3$ cups (8-ounce package) HEATH Milk Chocolate Toffee Bits

1. Heat oven to 350°F. Grease bottom of 8-inch square baking pan.

2. Melt butter and chocolate in medium saucepan over low heat, stirring occasionally. Stir in sugar. Add eggs, one at a time, beating after each addition. Stir in vanilla. Combine flour, baking powder and salt; add to chocolate mixture, stirring until well blended. Spread batter in prepared pan.

3. Bake 20 minutes or until brownie begins to pull away from sides of pan. Remove from oven; sprinkle with toffee bits. Cover tightly with foil and cool completely on wire rack. Remove foil; cut into squares.

Simply Special Brownies

Makes 20 brownies

$^1/_2$ **cup (1 stick) butter or margarine**

1 **package (4 ounces) HERSHEY'S SPECIAL DARK Premium Chocolate Baking Bar, broken into pieces**

2 **eggs**

1 **teaspoon vanilla extract**

$^3/_4$ **teaspoon powdered instant coffee**

$^2/_3$ **cup sugar**

$^1/_2$ **cup all-purpose flour**

$^1/_4$ **teaspoon baking soda**

$^1/_4$ **teaspoon salt**

$^1/_2$ **cup coarsely chopped nuts (optional)**

1. Heat oven to 350°F. Grease 9-inch square baking pan.

2. Place butter and chocolate in medium microwave-safe bowl. Microwave at MEDIUM (50%) 1 minute; stir. If necessary, microwave an additional 15 seconds at a time, stirring after each heating, until chocolate is melted and mixture is smooth when stirred. Add eggs, vanilla and instant coffee, stirring until well blended. Stir in sugar, flour, baking soda and salt; blend completely. Stir in nuts, if desired. Spread batter in prepared pan.

3. Bake 25 to 30 minutes or until wooden pick inserted in center comes out almost clean. Cool completely in pan on wire rack. Cut into bars.

Double Chip Brownies

Makes about 36 brownies

$3/4$ cup **HERSHEY'S Cocoa**

$1/2$ teaspoon **baking soda**

$2/3$ cup **butter or margarine, melted and divided**

$1/2$ cup **boiling water**

2 cups **sugar**

2 **eggs**

$1^1/3$ cups **all-purpose flour**

1 teaspoon **vanilla extract**

$1/4$ teaspoon **salt**

1 cup **HERSHEY'S Milk Chocolate Chips**

1 cup **REESE'S Peanut Butter Chips**

1. Heat oven to 350°F. Grease 13×9×2-inch baking pan.

2. Stir together cocoa and baking soda in large bowl; stir in $1/3$ cup melted butter. Add boiling water; stir until mixture thickens. Stir in sugar, eggs and remaining $1/3$ cup melted butter; stir until smooth. Add flour, vanilla and salt; blend thoroughly. Stir in milk chocolate chips and peanut butter chips. Spread in prepared pan.

3. Bake 35 to 40 minutes or until brownies begin to pull away from sides of pan. Cool completely in pan on wire rack. Cut into squares.

Butter Pecan Squares

Makes about 16 squares

$1/2$ cup (1 stick) **butter, softened**

$1/2$ cup packed **light brown sugar**

1 **egg**

1 teaspoon **vanilla extract**

$3/4$ cup **all-purpose flour**

2 cups (11.5-ounce package) **HERSHEY'S Milk Chocolate Chips, divided**

$3/4$ cup **chopped pecans, divided**

1. Heat oven to 350°F. Grease 8- or 9-inch square baking pan.

2. Beat butter, brown sugar, egg and vanilla in medium bowl until fluffy. Beat in flour. Stir in 1 cup milk chocolate chips and $1/2$ cup pecans. Spread in prepared pan.

3. Bake 25 to 30 minutes or until lightly browned. Remove from oven. Immediately sprinkle remaining 1 cup chips over surface. Let stand 5 to 10 minutes or until chips soften; spread evenly. Immediately sprinkle remaining $1/4$ cup pecans over top; press gently onto chocolate. Cool completely in pan on wire rack. Cut into squares.

Double Chip Brownies

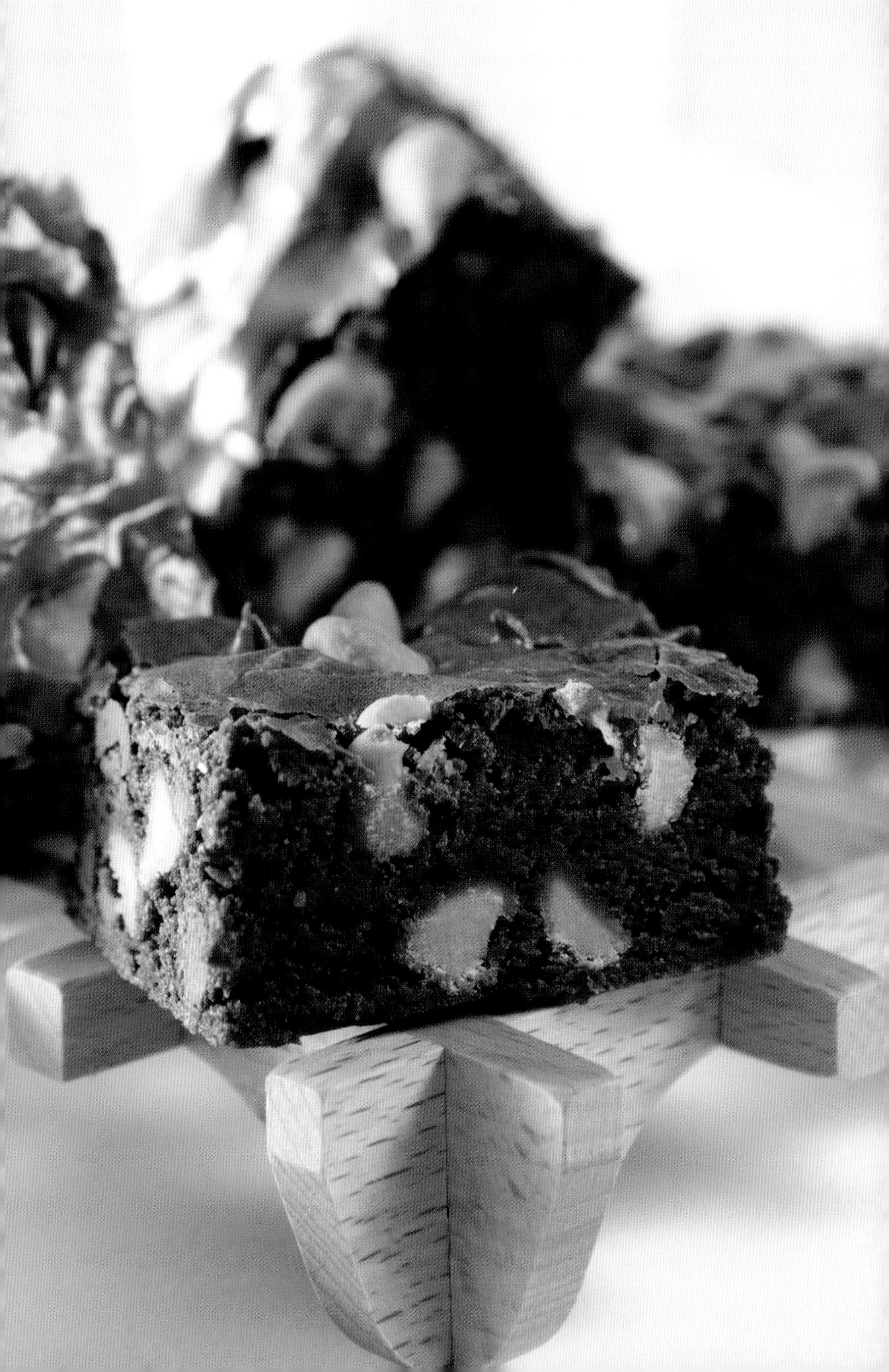

English Toffee Bars

Makes about 36 bars

44

- 2 **cups all-purpose flour**
- 1 **cup packed light brown sugar**
- $1/2$ **cup (1 stick) cold butter**
- 1 **cup pecan halves**
- **TOFFEE TOPPING (recipe follows)**
- 1 **cup HERSHEY'S Milk Chocolate Chips**

1. Heat oven to 350°F.

2. Combine flour, brown sugar and butter in large bowl; mix until fine crumbs form (a few large crumbs may remain).

Press into ungreased 13×9-inch baking pan. Sprinkle pecans over crust. Prepare TOFFEE TOPPING; drizzle evenly over pecans and crust.

3. Bake 20 to 22 minutes or until topping is bubbly and golden. Remove from oven. Immediately sprinkle milk chocolate chips over top; press gently onto surface. Cool completely. Cut into bars.

TOFFEE TOPPING: Combine $2/3$ cup butter and $1/3$ cup packed light brown sugar in small saucepan. Cook over medium heat, stirring constantly, until mixture comes to boil; boil and stir 30 seconds. Use immediately.

Peanut Butter Chips and Jelly Bars

Makes about 16 bars

- $1^1/2$ **cups all-purpose flour**
- $1/2$ **cup sugar**
- $3/4$ **teaspoon baking powder**
- $1/2$ **cup (1 stick) cold butter or margarine**
- 1 **egg, beaten**
- $3/4$ **cup grape jelly**
- $1^2/3$ **cups (10-ounce package) REESE'S Peanut Butter Chips, divided**

1. Heat oven to 375°F. Grease 9-inch square baking pan.

2. Stir together flour, sugar and baking powder in large bowl. Cut in butter with pastry blender or two knives until mixture resembles coarse crumbs. Add egg; blend well. Reserve 1 cup mixture; press remaining mixture onto bottom of prepared pan. Stir jelly to soften; spread evenly over crust. Sprinkle 1 cup peanut butter chips over jelly. Stir together reserved crumb mixture with remaining $2/3$ cup chips; sprinkle over top.

3. Bake 25 to 30 minutes or until lightly browned. Cool completely in pan on wire rack. Cut into bars.

English Toffee Bars

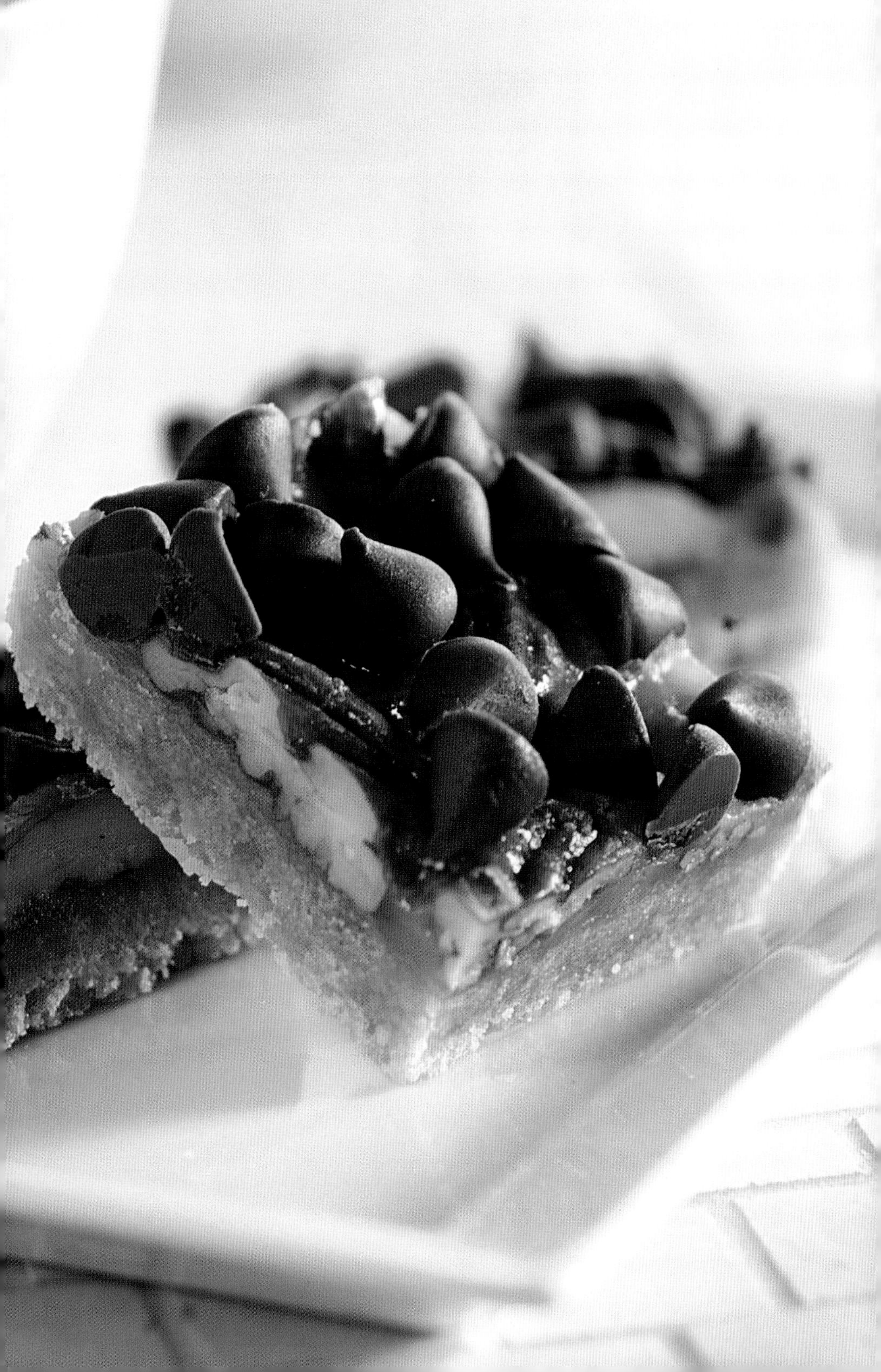

Perfectly Peppermint Brownies

Makes 36 brownies

$^3/_4$ **cup HERSHEY'S Cocoa**

$^1/_2$ **teaspoon baking soda**

$^2/_3$ **cup butter or margarine, melted and divided**

$^1/_2$ **cup boiling water**

2 **cups sugar**

2 **eggs**

$1^1/_3$ **cups all-purpose flour**

1 **teaspoon vanilla extract**

$^1/_4$ **teaspoon salt**

$1^1/_3$ **cups (8-ounce package) YORK Mini Peppermint Patties***

*16 to 17 small (1½-inch) YORK Peppermint Patties, unwrapped and coarsely chopped, may be substituted for the mini peppermint patties.

1. Heat oven to 350°F. Grease 13×9×2-inch baking pan.

2. Stir together cocoa and baking soda in large bowl; stir in $^1/_3$ cup butter. Add boiling water; stir until mixture thickens. Stir in sugar, eggs and remaining $^1/_3$ cup butter; stir until smooth. Add flour, vanilla and salt; blend completely. Stir in peppermint patties. Spread in prepared pan.

3. Bake 35 to 40 minutes or until brownies begin to pull away from sides of pan. Cool completely in pan on wire rack. Cut into bars.

Raspberry and Chocolate Streusel Bars

Makes 36 bars

$2^1/_2$ **cups all-purpose flour**

1 **cup sugar**

$^3/_4$ **cup finely chopped pecans**

1 **egg, beaten**

1 **cup (2 sticks) cold butter or margarine**

1 **jar (12 ounces) seedless red raspberry jam**

$1^1/_3$ **cups (8-ounce package) HERSHEY'S Dark Chocolate Baking Pieces Filled with Raspberry Crème**

1. Heat oven to 350°F. Grease 13×9×2-inch baking pan.

2. Stir together flour, sugar, pecans and egg in large bowl. Cut in butter with pastry blender or fork until mixture resembles coarse crumbs; set aside 1½ cups crumb mixture. Press remaining crumb mixture on bottom of prepared pan. Stir jam to soften; carefully spread over crumb mixture. Sprinkle with baking pieces. Crumble remaining crumb mixture evenly over top.

3. Bake 40 to 45 minutes or until lightly browned. Cool completely in pan on wire rack; cut into bars.

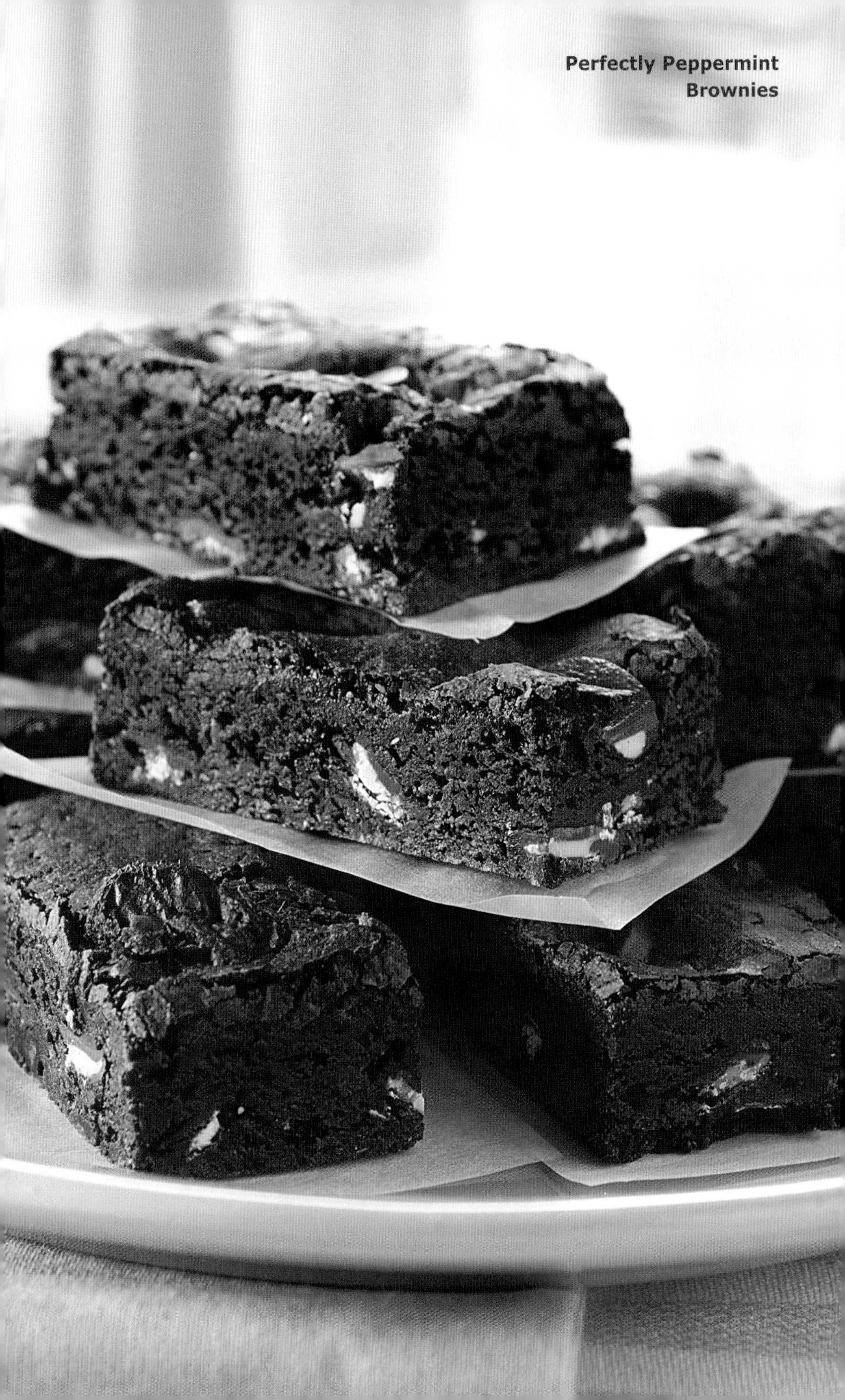
Perfectly Peppermint
Brownies

Chocolate Almond Macaroon Bars

Makes about 36 bars

48

2 **cups chocolate wafer cookie crumbs**

6 **tablespoons butter or margarine, melted**

6 **tablespoons powdered sugar**

1 **can (14 ounces) sweetened condensed milk (not evaporated milk)**

3³/₄ **cups MOUNDS Sweetened Coconut Flakes**

1 **cup sliced almonds, toasted* (optional)**

1 **cup HERSHEY'S SPECIAL DARK Chocolate Chips or HERSHEY'S Semi-Sweet Chocolate Chips**

¹/₄ **cup whipping cream**

¹/₂ **cup HERSHEY'S Premier White Chips**

*To toast almonds: Heat oven to 350°F. Spread almonds evenly on shallow baking sheet. Bake 5 to 8 minutes or until lightly browned.

1. Heat oven to 350°F. Grease 13×9×2-inch baking pan.

2. Combine crumbs, melted butter and sugar in large bowl. Firmly press crumb mixture on bottom of prepared pan. Stir together sweetened condensed milk, coconut and almonds in large bowl, mixing well. Carefully drop mixture by spoonfuls over crust; spread evenly.

3. Bake 20 to 25 minutes or until coconut edges just begin to brown. Cool.

4. Place chocolate chips and whipping cream in medium microwave-safe bowl. Microwave at MEDIUM (50%) 1 minute; stir. If necessary, microwave at MEDIUM an additional 10 seconds at a time, stirring after each heating, until chips are melted and mixture is smooth when stirred. Cool until slightly thickened; spread over cooled bars. Sprinkle top with white chips. Cover; refrigerate several hours or until thoroughly chilled. Cut into bars. Refrigerate leftovers.

Chewy Toffee Almond Bars

Makes 36 bars

1   cup (2 sticks) butter,
    softened

$1/2$ cup sugar

2   cups all-purpose flour

$1^{1/3}$ cups (8-ounce package)
    HEATH BITS 'O BRICKLE
    Toffee Bits

$3/4$ cup light corn syrup

1   cup sliced almonds,
    divided

$3/4$ cup MOUNDS Sweetened
    Coconut Flakes, divided

1. Heat oven to 350°F. Grease sides of 13×9×2-inch baking pan.

2. Beat butter and sugar with electric mixer on medium speed in large bowl until fluffy. Gradually add flour, beating until well blended. Press dough evenly in prepared pan. Bake 15 to 20 minutes or until edges are lightly browned.

3. Meanwhile, combine toffee bits and corn syrup in medium saucepan. Cook over medium heat, stirring constantly, until toffee is melted (about 10 to 12 minutes). Stir in $1/2$ cup almonds and $1/2$ cup coconut. Spread toffee mixture to within $1/4$ inch of edges of crust. Sprinkle remaining $1/2$ cup almonds and remaining $1/4$ cup coconut over top.

4. Bake an additional 15 minutes or until bubbly. Cool completely in pan on wire rack. Cut into bars.

Layered Cookie Bars

Makes about 36 bars

3/4 cup (1^1/2 sticks) butter or margarine

1^3/4 cups vanilla wafer crumbs

6 tablespoons HERSHEY'S Cocoa

1/4 cup sugar

1 can (14 ounces) sweetened condensed milk (not evaporated milk)

1 cup HERSHEY'S SPECIAL DARK Chocolate Chips or HERSHEY'S Semi-Sweet Chocolate Chips

3/4 cup HEATH BITS 'O BRICKLE Toffee Bits

1 cup chopped walnuts

1. Heat oven to 350°F. Melt butter in 13×9×2-inch baking pan in oven. Combine crumbs, cocoa and sugar; sprinkle over butter.

2. Pour sweetened condensed milk evenly on top of crumbs. Top with chocolate chips and toffee bits, then nuts; press down firmly.

3. Bake 25 to 30 minutes or until lightly browned. Cool completely in pan on wire rack. Chill, if desired. Cut into bars. Store covered at room temperature.

Championship Chocolate Chip Bars

Makes about 36 bars

1^1/$_2$ cups all-purpose flour

^{1}/$_2$ cup packed light brown sugar

^{1}/$_2$ cup (1 stick) cold butter or margarine

2 cups (12-ounce package) HERSHEY'S SPECIAL DARK Chocolate Chips or HERSHEY'S Semi-Sweet Chocolate Chips, divided

1 can (14 ounces) sweetened condensed milk (not evaporated milk)

1 egg

1 teaspoon vanilla extract

1 cup chopped nuts

1. Heat oven to 350°F.

2. Stir together flour and brown sugar in medium bowl; with pastry blender, cut in butter until mixture resembles coarse crumbs. Stir in ^{1}/$_2$ cup chocolate chips; press mixture onto bottom of 13×9×2-inch baking pan. Bake 15 minutes.

3. Meanwhile, in large bowl, combine sweetened condensed milk, egg and vanilla. Stir in remaining 1^1/$_2$ cups chips and nuts. Spread over baked crust. Continue baking 25 minutes or until golden brown. Cool completely in pan on wire rack. Cut into bars.

Chippy Chewy Bars

Makes about 48 bars

1/2 cup (1 stick) butter or margarine

1 1/2 cups graham cracker crumbs

1 2/3 cups (10-ounce package) REESE'S Peanut Butter Chips, divided

1 1/2 cups MOUNDS Sweetened Coconut Flakes

1 can (14 ounces) sweetened condensed milk (not evaporated milk)

1 cup HERSHEY'S SPECIAL DARK Chocolate Chips, HERSHEY'S Semi-Sweet Chocolate Chips or HERSHEY'S Mini Chips Semi-Sweet Chocolate

1 1/2 teaspoons shortening (do not use butter, margarine, spread or oil)

1. Heat oven to 350°F.

2. Place butter in 13×9×2-inch baking pan. Heat in oven until melted. Remove pan from oven. Sprinkle graham cracker crumbs evenly over butter; press down with fork. Layer 1 cup peanut butter chips over crumbs; sprinkle coconut over peanut butter chips. Layer remaining 2/3 cup peanut butter chips over coconut; drizzle sweetened condensed milk evenly over top. Press down firmly.

3. Bake 20 minutes or until lightly browned.

4. Place chocolate chips and shortening in small microwave-safe bowl. Microwave at MEDIUM (50%) 1 minute; stir. If necessary, microwave at MEDIUM an additional 15 seconds at a time, stirring after each heating, just until chips are melted when stirred. Drizzle evenly over top of baked mixture. Cool completely in pan on wire rack. Cut into bars.

Note: For lighter drizzle, use 1/2 cup chocolate chips and 3/4 teaspoon shortening. Microwave at MEDIUM (50%) 30 seconds to 1 minute; stir. If necessary, microwave at MEDIUM an additional 15 seconds at a time, stirring after each heating, just until chips are melted when stirred.

Peanut Butter Fudge Brownie Bars

Makes 36 bars

1 cup (2 sticks) butter or margarine, melted

1¹/₂ cups sugar

2 eggs

1 teaspoon vanilla extract

1¹/₄ cups all-purpose flour

²/₃ cup HERSHEY'S Cocoa

¹/₄ cup milk

1¹/₄ cups chopped pecans or walnuts, divided

¹/₂ cup (1 stick) butter or margarine

1²/₃ cups (10-ounce package) REESE'S Peanut Butter Chips

1 can (14 ounces) sweetened condensed milk (not evaporated milk)

¹/₄ cup HERSHEY'S SPECIAL DARK Chocolate Chips or HERSHEY'S Semi-Sweet Chocolate Chips

1. Heat oven to 350°F. Grease 13×9×2-inch baking pan.

2. Beat melted butter, sugar, eggs and vanilla in large bowl with electric mixer on medium speed until well blended. Add flour, cocoa and milk; beat until blended. Stir in 1 cup nuts. Spread in prepared pan.

3. Bake 25 to 30 minutes or just until edges begin to pull away from sides of pan. Cool completely in pan on wire rack.

4. Melt ¹/₂ cup butter and peanut butter chips in medium saucepan over low heat, stirring constantly. Add sweetened condensed milk, stirring until smooth; pour over baked layer.

5. Place chocolate chips in small microwave-safe bowl. Microwave at MEDIUM (50%) 45 seconds or just until chips are melted when stirred. Drizzle bars with melted chocolate; sprinkle with remaining ¹/₄ cup nuts. Refrigerate 1 hour or until firm. Cut into bars. Cover; refrigerate leftover bars.

Rocky Road Tasty Team Treats
Makes about 36 bars

1½ cups finely crushed thin pretzels or pretzel sticks

¾ cup (1½ sticks) butter or margarine, melted

1 can (14 ounces) sweetened condensed milk (not evaporated milk)

1¾ cups (10-ounce package) HERSHEY'S MINI KISSES BRAND Milk Chocolates

3 cups miniature marshmallows

1⅓ cups coarsely chopped pecans or pecan pieces

1. Heat oven to 350°F. Grease bottom and sides of 13×9×2-inch baking pan.

2. Combine pretzels and melted butter in small bowl; press evenly onto bottom of prepared pan. Spread sweetened condensed milk evenly over pretzel layer; layer evenly with chocolates, marshmallows and pecans, in order. Press down firmly on pecans.

3. Bake 20 to 25 minutes or until lightly browned. Cool completely in pan on wire rack. Cut into bars.

Oatmeal Toffee Bars
Makes about 36 bars

1 cup (2 sticks) butter or margarine, softened

1 cup packed light brown sugar

2 eggs

1 teaspoon vanilla extract

1½ cups all-purpose flour

1 teaspoon baking soda

½ teaspoon ground cinnamon

½ teaspoon salt

1⅓ cups (8-ounce package) HEATH BITS 'O BRICKLE Toffee Bits, divided

3 cups quick-cooking or regular rolled oats

1. Heat oven to 350°F. Grease 13×9×2-inch baking pan.

2. Beat butter and brown sugar in large bowl until well blended. Add eggs and vanilla; beat well. Stir together flour, baking soda, cinnamon and salt; gradually add to butter mixture, beating until well blended. Set aside ¼ cup toffee bits. Stir remaining toffee bits and oats into batter (batter will be stiff). Spread batter in prepared pan; sprinkle reserved ¼ cup toffee bits over surface.

3. Bake 25 minutes or until wooden pick inserted in center comes out clean. Cool completely in pan on wire rack. Cut into bars.

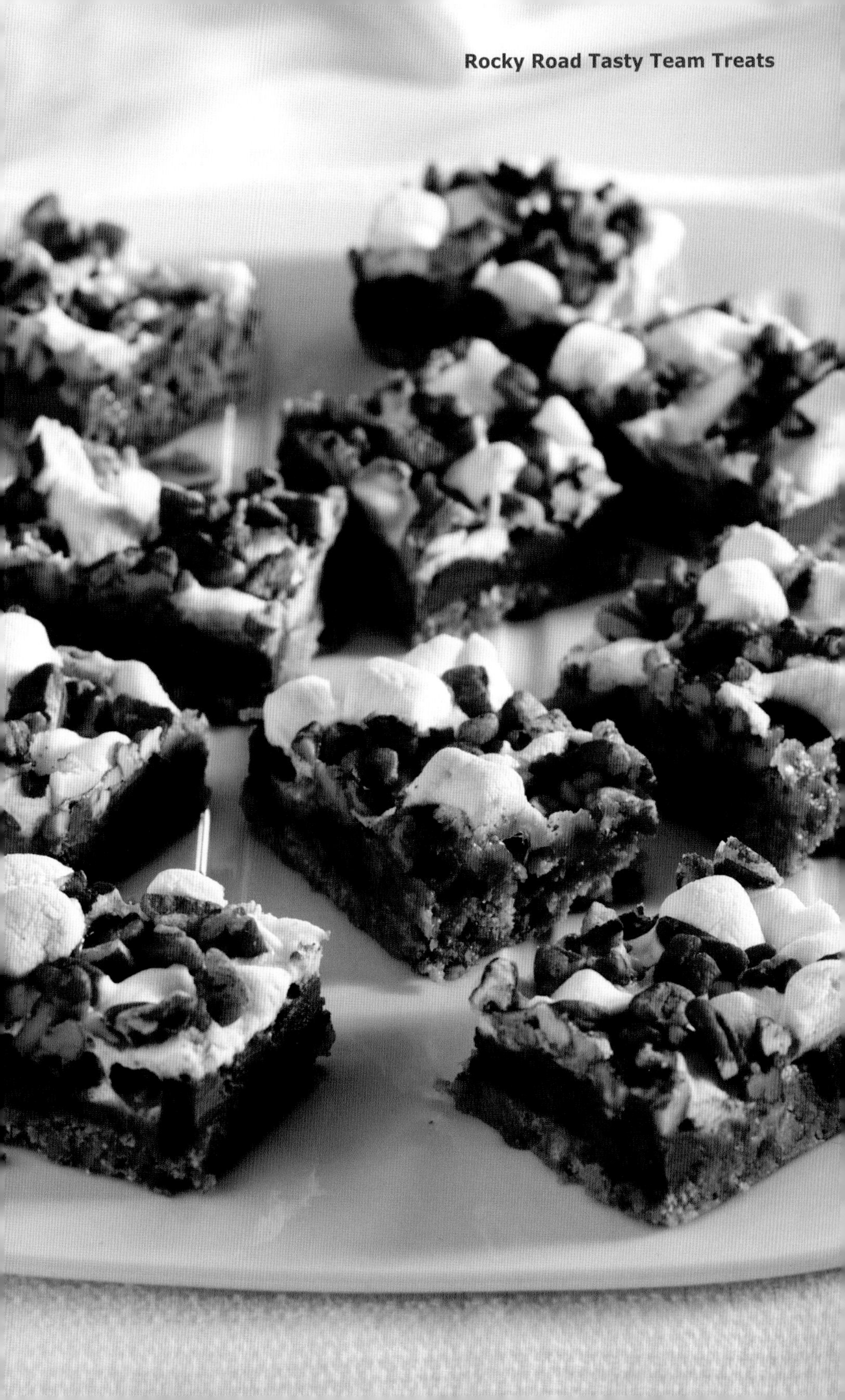

Rocky Road Tasty Team Treats

Quarterback Blitz Bars

Makes about 36 bars

1 cup (2 sticks) butter or margarine

2¼ cups graham cracker crumbs

⅓ cup HERSHEY'S Cocoa

3 tablespoons sugar

1 can (14 ounces) sweetened condensed milk (not evaporated milk)

1 cup HERSHEY'S MINI KISSES BRAND Milk Chocolates

1 cup HEATH BITS 'O BRICKLE Toffee Bits

1 cup chopped walnuts

1 cup MOUNDS Sweetened Coconut Flakes

1. Heat oven to 350°F. Place butter in 13×9×2-inch baking pan; heat in oven until melted. Remove from oven.

2. Stir together graham cracker crumbs, cocoa and sugar; sprinkle over melted butter. Stir mixture until evenly coated; press evenly with spatula onto bottom of pan. Pour sweetened condensed milk evenly over crumb mixture. Sprinkle with chocolate pieces and toffee bits. Sprinkle nuts and coconut on top; press down firmly.

3. Bake 25 to 30 minutes or until lightly browned. Cool completely in pan on wire rack. Cover with foil; let stand at room temperature several hours. Cut into bars.

CAKES & CHEESECAKES

Autumn Peanutty Carrot Cake

Makes 10 to 12 servings

3 **eggs**

³/₄ **cup vegetable oil**

1 **teaspoon vanilla extract**

1¹/₂ **cups all-purpose flour**

³/₄ **cup granulated sugar**

¹/₂ **cup packed light brown sugar**

2 **teaspoons ground cinnamon**

1¹/₄ **teaspoons baking soda**

2 **cups grated carrots**

1²/₃ **cups (10-ounce package) REESE'S Peanut Butter Chips**

¹/₂ **cup chopped walnuts**

CREAM CHEESE FROSTING (recipe follows)

1. Heat oven to 350°F. Grease and flour 2 (8-inch) round baking pans.

2. Beat eggs, oil and vanilla in large bowl. Stir together flour, granulated sugar, brown sugar, cinnamon and baking soda; add to egg mixture and blend well. Stir in carrots, peanut butter chips and walnuts; pour into prepared pans.

3. Bake 30 to 35 minutes or until wooden pick inserted in centers comes out clean. Cool 10 minutes; remove from pans to wire rack. Cool completely. Frost with CREAM CHEESE FROSTING. Cover; refrigerate leftover cake.

CREAM CHEESE FROSTING: Beat 2 packages (3 ounces each) softened cream cheese and ¹/₂ cup (1 stick) softened butter until smooth. Gradually add 4 cups powdered sugar and 2 teaspoons vanilla extract, beating until smooth.

Chocolate Syrup Swirl Cake

Makes 20 servings

1 cup (2 sticks) butter or margarine, softened

2 cups sugar

2 teaspoons vanilla extract

3 eggs

2³/₄ cups all-purpose flour

1¹/₄ teaspoons baking soda, divided

¹/₂ teaspoon salt

1 cup buttermilk or sour milk*

1 cup HERSHEY'S Syrup

1 cup MOUNDS Sweetened Coconut Flakes (optional)

***To sour milk:** Use 1 tablespoon white vinegar plus milk to equal 1 cup.*

1. Heat oven to 350°F. Grease and flour 12-cup fluted tube pan or 10-inch tube pan.

2. Beat butter, sugar and vanilla in large bowl until fluffy. Add eggs; beat well. Stir together flour, 1 teaspoon baking soda and salt; add alternately with buttermilk to butter mixture, beating until well blended.

3. Measure 2 cups batter in small bowl; stir in syrup and remaining ¹/₄ teaspoon baking soda. Add coconut, if desired, to remaining vanilla batter; pour into prepared pan. Pour chocolate batter over vanilla batter in pan; do not mix.

4. Bake 60 to 70 minutes or until wooden pick inserted in center comes out clean. Cool 15 minutes; remove from pan to wire rack. Cool completely; glaze or frost as desired.

Brownie Cheesecake

Makes 10 to 12 servings

1 cup ³/₄-inch brownie pieces (recipe follows)

CHOCOLATE CRUMB CRUST (recipe follows)

4 packages (8 ounces each) cream cheese, softened

1 cup sugar

1¹/₂ teaspoons vanilla extract

4 eggs

1. Prepare brownie using recipe below or your own favorite recipe.

2. Heat oven to 350°F. Prepare CHOCOLATE CRUMB CRUST; cool slightly. Beat cream cheese, sugar and vanilla until smooth. Gradually add eggs, beating well after each addition. Pour batter into prepared crust.

3. Sprinkle brownie pieces over cheesecake surface; push pieces into batter, covering completely. Bake 50 to 55 minutes or until almost set.* Remove from oven to wire rack. With knife, loosen cake from side of pan; cool.

4. Cover; refrigerate. Just before serving, garnish as desired. Cover; refrigerate leftover cheesecake.

Cheesecakes are less likely to crack if baked in a water bath.

BEST BROWNIES

¹/₂ cup (1 stick) butter or margarine, melted

1 cup sugar

1 teaspoon vanilla extract

2 eggs

¹/₂ cup all-purpose flour

¹/₃ cup HERSHEY'S Cocoa

¹/₄ teaspoon baking powder

¹/₄ teaspoon salt

Heat oven to 350°F. Grease 8- or 9-inch square baking pan. Stir together butter, sugar and vanilla in bowl. Add eggs; beat well with spoon. Stir together flour, cocoa, baking powder and salt; gradually add to egg mixture, beating until well blended. Spread batter in prepared pan. Bake 20 to 25 minutes or until brownies begin to pull away from sides of pan. Cool completely in pan on wire rack.

CHOCOLATE CRUMB CRUST: Heat oven to 350°F. Combine 1¹/₂ cups (about 45 wafers) vanilla wafer crumbs, 6 tablespoons powdered sugar, 6 tablespoons HERSHEY'S Cocoa and 6 tablespoons butter or margarine (melted). Press crumb mixture onto bottom and ¹/₂ to 1 inch up side of 9-inch springform pan. Bake 8 minutes; cool slightly.

Chocolate & Peanut Butter Fudge Cheesecake

Makes 10 to 12 servings

1¹/₂ cups vanilla wafer crumbs (about 45 wafers, crushed)

¹/₂ cup powdered sugar

¹/₄ cup HERSHEY'S Cocoa

¹/₃ cup butter or margarine, melted

3 packages (8 ounces each) cream cheese, softened

³/₄ cup granulated sugar

3 eggs

¹/₃ cup dairy sour cream

3 tablespoons all-purpose flour

1 teaspoon vanilla extract

¹/₄ teaspoon salt

1 cup HERSHEY'S SPECIAL DARK Chocolate Chips or HERSHEY'S Semi-Sweet Chocolate Chips, melted

1 cup REESE'S Peanut Butter Chips, melted

HERSHEY'S Fudge Topping (optional)

Sweetened Whipped Cream (optional)

1. Heat oven to 350°F. Combine vanilla wafer crumbs, powdered sugar, cocoa and melted butter in medium bowl. Press onto bottom and 1 inch up side of 9-inch springform pan. Bake 8 minutes; cool.

2. Beat cream cheese and granulated sugar in large bowl until smooth. Add eggs, sour cream, flour, vanilla and salt; beat until well blended.

3. Place half of batter in separate bowl. Stir melted chocolate into one bowl of cream cheese mixture and melted peanut butter chips into the other. Spread chocolate mixture in prepared crust. Gently spread peanut butter mixture over chocolate mixture. Do not stir.

4. Bake 50 to 55 minutes or until center is almost set. (For less cracking of cheesecake surface, bake in water bath.) Remove from oven to wire rack. With knife, loosen cake from side of pan. Cool completely; remove side of pan. Cover; refrigerate.

5. To serve, drizzle each slice with fudge topping and top with whipped cream, if desired. Cover; refrigerate leftover cheesecake.

Spicy Butterscotch Snack Cake

Makes 12 to 16 servings

1 cup (2 sticks) butter or margarine, softened

1 cup sugar

2 eggs

1/2 teaspoon vanilla extract

1/2 cup applesauce

2 1/2 cups all-purpose flour

1 1/2 to 2 teaspoons ground cinnamon

1 teaspoon baking soda

1/2 teaspoon salt

1 3/4 cups (11-ounce package) HERSHEY'S Butterscotch Chips

1 cup chopped pecans (optional)

Powdered sugar or frozen whipped topping, thawed (optional)

1. Heat oven to 350°F. Lightly grease 13×9×2-inch baking pan.

2. Beat butter and sugar in large bowl until fluffy. Add eggs and vanilla; beat well. Mix in applesauce. Stir together flour, cinnamon, baking soda and salt; gradually add to butter mixture, beating until well blended. Stir in butterscotch chips and pecans, if desired. Spread in prepared pan.

3. Bake 35 to 40 minutes or until wooden pick inserted in center comes out clean. Cool completely in pan. Dust with powdered sugar or serve with whipped topping, if desired.

Petit Mocha Cheesecakes

Makes 42 cheesecakes

CRUMB CRUST
(recipe follows)

1 package (8 ounces)
cream cheese, softened

1 cup sugar

2 eggs

1 teaspoon vanilla extract

1/3 cup HERSHEY'S Cocoa

2 tablespoons all-purpose
flour

1 tablespoon powdered
instant coffee

1 teaspoon hot water

CHOCOLATE GLAZE
(recipe follows, optional)

1. Heat oven to 375°F. Line small muffin cups (1³/₄ inches in diameter) with paper baking cups.

2. Prepare CRUMB CRUST. Place 1 slightly heaping teaspoon crumb mixture into each cup; press lightly. Beat cream cheese in large bowl until fluffy. Add sugar, eggs and vanilla; beat well. Add cocoa and flour; beat well. Dissolve coffee in water; add to chocolate mixture. Place about 1 tablespoon chocolate mixture into each cup.

3. Bake 15 to 18 minutes or until just set. Cool completely in pan on wire rack. Drizzle with CHOCOLATE GLAZE, if desired. Refrigerate until cold, about 2 hours. Cover; refrigerate leftover cheesecakes.

CRUMB CRUST: Stir together ¹/₂ cup graham cracker crumbs, 2 tablespoons powdered sugar and 2 tablespoons melted butter or margarine in small bowl until well combined.

CHOCOLATE GLAZE: Combine ¹/₄ cup HERSHEY'S SPECIAL DARK Chocolate Chips or HERSHEY'S Semi-Sweet Chocolate Chips and 2 tablespoons whipping cream in small saucepan. Cook over very low heat, stirring constantly, until smooth. Use immediately.

Chocolate Bar Cake

Makes 10 to 12 servings

1¹/₃ cups (8-ounce package) HERSHEY'S Mini Milk Chocolate Bars,* divided

¹/₂ cup (1 stick) butter or margarine, softened

1 cup boiling water

2 cups all-purpose flour

1¹/₂ cups sugar

¹/₂ cup HERSHEY'S Cocoa

2 teaspoons baking soda

1 teaspoon salt

2 eggs

¹/₂ cup dairy sour cream

1 teaspoon vanilla extract

VANILLA GLAZE (recipe follows)

*6 HERSHEY'S Milk Chocolate Bars (1.55 ounces each) may be substituted for the mini milk chocolate bars. Reserve 1 bar for garnish; proceed as above.

1. Heat oven to 350°F. Grease and flour 12-cup fluted tube pan. Set aside 2 tablespoons chocolate bars for garnish.

2. Stir together remaining chocolate bars, butter and water in small bowl until chocolate is melted. Stir together flour, sugar, cocoa, baking soda and salt in large bowl; gradually add chocolate mixture, beating on medium speed of mixer until well blended. Add eggs, sour cream and vanilla; blend well. Beat 1 minute. Pour batter into prepared pan.

3. Bake 50 to 55 minutes or until wooden pick inserted in center comes out clean. Cool 10 minutes; remove from pan to wire rack. Cool completely. Prepare VANILLA GLAZE; drizzle over cake. Decorate top of cake with reserved chocolate bars.

VANILLA GLAZE

¹/₄ cup (¹/₂ stick) butter or margarine

2 cups powdered sugar

2 tablespoons hot water

1 teaspoon vanilla extract

1. Place butter in medium microwave-safe bowl. Microwave at MEDIUM (50%) 30 seconds or until melted.

2. Gradually stir in powdered sugar, water and vanilla, beating with whisk until smooth and slightly thickened. Add additional water, 1 teaspoon at a time, if needed.

Chocolate Almond Cheesecake

Makes 10 to 12 servings

ALMOND CRUMB CRUST
(recipe follows)

3 **packages (8 ounces each)**
cream cheese, softened

1$^1/_4$ **cups sugar**

$^1/_2$ **cup dairy sour cream**

$^1/_3$ **cup HERSHEY'S Cocoa**

2 **tablespoons all-purpose**
flour

3 **eggs**

2 **teaspoons almond extract**

1 **teaspoon vanilla extract**

ALMOND WHIPPED CREAM
(recipe follows)

Sliced almonds (optional)

1. Prepare ALMOND CRUMB
CRUST.

2. Increase oven temperature to
425°F. Combine cream cheese,
sugar, sour cream, cocoa and
flour in large bowl; beat with
electric mixer on medium speed
until smooth. Add eggs, almond
extract and vanilla; beat well.
Pour into prepared crust.

3. Bake 10 minutes. Reduce oven
temperature to 250°F; continue
baking 55 minutes or until center
appears set. Remove from oven
to wire rack. With knife, loosen
cake from side of pan. Cool
completely; remove side of pan.

4. Refrigerate several hours
before serving. Garnish with
ALMOND WHIPPED CREAM and
sliced almonds, if desired. Cover;
refrigerate leftover cheesecake.

ALMOND CRUMB CRUST: Heat
oven to 350°F. Stir together
$^3/_4$ cup vanilla wafer crumbs
(about 20 wafers), $^1/_2$ cup
ground blanched almonds and
3 tablespoons sugar in small
bowl; stir in 3 tablespoons
melted butter or margarine.
Press mixture firmly onto
bottom and $^1/_2$ inch up side
of 9-inch springform pan. Bake
8 to 10 minutes; cool slightly.

ALMOND WHIPPED CREAM:
Combine $^1/_2$ cup cold whipping
cream, 2 tablespoons powdered
sugar, $^1/_4$ teaspoon vanilla extract
and $^1/_8$ teaspoon almond extract
in small bowl; beat until stiff.
Makes 1 cup whipped cream.

Nutty Toffee Coffee Cake

Makes 12 to 16 servings

1^{1}/$_{3}$ cups (8-ounce package) **HEATH BITS 'O BRICKLE Toffee Bits, divided**

^{1}/$_{3}$ cup plus ^{3}/$_{4}$ cup packed **light brown sugar, divided**

2^{1}/$_{4}$ cups all-purpose flour, **divided**

9 tablespoons butter or **margarine, softened and divided**

^{3}/$_{4}$ cup granulated sugar

2 teaspoons baking powder

^{1}/$_{2}$ teaspoon ground cinnamon

^{1}/$_{4}$ teaspoon salt

1^{1}/$_{4}$ cups milk

1 egg

1 teaspoon vanilla extract

^{3}/$_{4}$ cup chopped nuts

1. Heat oven to 350°F. Grease and flour 13×9×2-inch baking pan. Stir together ^{1}/$_{2}$ cup toffee bits, ^{1}/$_{3}$ cup brown sugar, ^{1}/$_{4}$ cup flour and 3 tablespoons butter. Stir until crumbly; set aside.

2. Combine remaining 2 cups flour, granulated sugar, remaining ^{3}/$_{4}$ cup brown sugar, remaining 6 tablespoons butter, baking powder, cinnamon and salt in large mixer bowl; mix until well blended. Gradually add milk, egg and vanilla, beating until thoroughly blended. Stir in remaining toffee bits and nuts. Spread batter in prepared pan.

3. Sprinkle reserved crumb topping over batter. Bake 30 to 35 minutes or until wooden pick inserted in center comes out clean. Cool. Serve warm or cool.

White Chip and Macadamia Nut Coffeecake

Makes 12 to 16 servings

CRUMB TOPPING
(recipe follows)

6 tablespoons butter or margarine, softened

$3/4$ cup granulated sugar

$3/4$ cup packed light brown sugar

2 cups all-purpose flour

2 teaspoons baking powder

$1/2$ teaspoon ground cinnamon

$1^1/4$ cups milk

1 egg

1 teaspoon vanilla extract

WHITE DRIZZLE
(recipe follows)

1. Heat oven to 350°F. Grease and flour 13×9×2-inch baking pan. Prepare CRUMB TOPPING; set aside.

2. Beat butter, granulated sugar and brown sugar until well blended. Stir together flour, baking powder and cinnamon; beat into butter mixture. Gradually add milk, egg and vanilla, beating until thoroughly blended. Pour $1/2$ batter into prepared pan; top with $1/2$ CRUMB TOPPING. Gently spread remaining batter over topping. Sprinkle remaining topping over batter.

3. Bake 30 to 35 minutes or until wooden pick inserted into center comes out clean. Cool completely.

4. Prepare WHITE DRIZZLE; drizzle over cake.

CRUMB TOPPING: Combine $2/3$ cup packed light brown sugar, $1/2$ cup all-purpose flour, 6 tablespoons firm butter or margarine and 1 cup HERSHEY'S Premier White Chips and $1/2$ cup MAUNA LOA Macadamia Nut Baking Pieces in medium bowl. Mix until crumbly.

WHITE DRIZZLE: Beat together $3/4$ cup powdered sugar, 2 to 3 teaspoons milk, 1 teaspoon softened butter and $1/4$ teaspoon vanilla extract. If necessary, stir in additional milk $1/2$ teaspoon at a time until desired consistency.

HERSHEY'S "PERFECTLY CHOCOLATE" Chocolate Cake

Makes 10 to 12 servings

2 cups sugar

1³/₄ cups all-purpose flour

³/₄ cup HERSHEY'S Cocoa

1¹/₂ teaspoons baking powder

1¹/₂ teaspoons baking soda

1 teaspoon salt

2 eggs

1 cup milk

¹/₂ cup vegetable oil

2 teaspoons vanilla extract

1 cup boiling water

"PERFECTLY CHOCOLATE"
CHOCOLATE FROSTING
(recipe follows)

1. Heat oven to 350°F. Grease and flour two 9-inch round baking pans.

2. Stir together sugar, flour, cocoa, baking powder, baking soda and salt in large bowl. Add eggs, milk, oil and vanilla; beat on medium speed of mixer 2 minutes. Stir in boiling water (batter will be thin). Pour batter evenly into prepared pans.

3. Bake 30 to 35 minutes or until wooden pick inserted into centers comes out clean. Cool 10 minutes; remove from pans to wire racks. Cool completely. Frost with "PERFECTLY CHOCOLATE" CHOCOLATE FROSTING.

One-Pan Cake: Grease and flour 13×9×2-inch baking pan. Heat oven to 350°F. Pour batter into prepared pan. Bake 35 to 40 minutes. Cool completely. Frost.

Three-Layer Cake: Grease and flour three 8-inch round baking pans. Heat oven to 350°F. Pour batter into prepared pans. Bake 30 to 35 minutes. Cool 10 minutes; remove from pans to wire racks. Cool completely. Frost.

Bundt Cake: Grease and flour 12-cup fluted tube pan. Heat oven to 350°F. Pour batter into prepared pan. Bake 50 to 55 minutes. Cool 15 minutes; remove from pan to wire rack. Cool completely. Frost.

Cupcakes: Line muffin cups (2¹/₂ inches in diameter) with paper bake cups. Heat oven to 350°F. Fill cups ²/₃ full with batter. Bake 22 to 25 minutes. Cool completely. Frost. Makes about 30 cupcakes.

"PERFECTLY CHOCOLATE" CHOCOLATE FROSTING

1 stick (¹/₂ cup) butter or margarine

²/₃ cup HERSHEY'S Cocoa

3 cups powdered sugar

¹/₃ cup milk

1 teaspoon vanilla extract

Melt butter. Stir in cocoa. Alternately add powdered sugar and milk, beating to spreading consistency. Add small amount additional milk, if needed. Stir in vanilla.

Makes about 2 cups frosting

Hot Fudge Pudding Cake

Makes about 8 servings

1$^1/_4$ **cups granulated sugar, divided**

1 **cup all-purpose flour**

$^1/_2$ **cup HERSHEY'S Cocoa, divided**

2 **teaspoons baking powder**

$^1/_4$ **teaspoon salt**

$^1/_2$ **cup milk**

$^1/_3$ **cup butter or margarine, melted**

1$^1/_2$ **teaspoons vanilla extract**

$^1/_2$ **cup packed light brown sugar**

1$^1/_4$ **cups hot water**

Whipped topping

1. Heat oven to 350°F. Stir together $^3/_4$ cup granulated sugar, flour, $^1/_4$ cup cocoa, baking powder and salt. Stir in milk, butter and vanilla; beat until smooth.

2. Pour batter into ungreased 9-inch square baking pan. Stir together remaining $^1/_2$ cup granulated sugar, brown sugar and remaining $^1/_4$ cup cocoa; sprinkle mixture evenly over batter. Pour hot water over top. Do not stir.

3. Bake 35 to 40 minutes or until center is almost set. Let stand 15 minutes; spoon into dessert dishes, spooning sauce from bottom of pan over top. Garnish with whipped topping.

Chocolate Streusel Coffeecake

Makes 12 to 16 servings

CHOCOLATE STREUSEL (recipe follows)

1/2 **cup (1 stick) butter or margarine, softened**

1 **cup sugar**

3 **eggs**

1 **container (8 ounces) dairy sour cream**

1 **teaspoon vanilla extract**

2 **cups all-purpose flour**

1 **teaspoon baking powder**

1 **teaspoon baking soda**

1/4 **teaspoon salt**

1. Heat oven to 350°F. Grease and flour 12-cup fluted tube pan. Prepare CHOCOLATE STREUSEL; set aside.

2. Beat butter and sugar in large bowl until fluffy. Add eggs; blend well on low speed of mixer. Stir in sour cream and vanilla. Combine flour, baking powder, baking soda and salt in separate bowl; add to batter. Blend well.

3. Sprinkle 1 cup CHOCOLATE STREUSEL into prepared pan. Spread 1/3 of the batter (about 1 1/3 cups) in pan; sprinkle with half the remaining streusel (about 1 cup). Repeat layers, ending with batter on top.

4. Bake 50 to 55 minutes or until wooden pick inserted near center comes out clean. Cool 10 minutes; invert onto serving plate. Cool completely.

CHOCOLATE STREUSEL

3/4 **cup packed light brown sugar**

1/4 **cup all-purpose flour**

1/4 **cup (1/2 stick) butter or margarine, softened**

3/4 **cup chopped nuts**

3/4 **cup HERSHEY'S Mini Chips Semi-Sweet Chocolate**

Combine brown sugar, flour and butter in medium bowl until crumbly. Stir in nuts and small chocolate chips.

Orange-Glazed Cocoa Bundt Cake

Makes 12 to 14 servings

$^3/_4$ cup (1$^1/_2$ sticks) butter or margarine, softened

1$^2/_3$ cups sugar

2 eggs

1 teaspoon vanilla extract

$^3/_4$ cup dairy sour cream

2 cups all-purpose flour

$^2/_3$ cup HERSHEY'S Cocoa

$^1/_2$ teaspoon salt

2 teaspoons baking soda

1 cup buttermilk or sour milk*

ORANGE GLAZE or
VANILLA GLAZE
(recipes follow)

*To sour milk: Use 1 tablespoon white vinegar plus milk to equal 1 cup.

1. Heat oven to 350°F. Grease and flour 12-cup fluted tube pan.

2. Beat butter, sugar, eggs and vanilla in large bowl until light and fluffy; stir in sour cream. Stir together flour, cocoa and salt. Stir baking soda into buttermilk in medium bowl; add alternately with dry ingredients to butter mixture. Beat 2 minutes on medium speed. Pour batter into prepared pan.

3. Bake 50 minutes or until wooden pick inserted into center comes out clean. Cool in pan 10 minutes. Remove from pan to wire rack. Cool completely. Glaze with ORANGE GLAZE; garnish as desired.

ORANGE GLAZE: Combine 2 cups powdered sugar, $^1/_4$ cup ($^1/_2$ stick) melted butter or margarine, 3 tablespoons orange juice, 1 teaspoon vanilla extract and $^1/_2$ teaspoon freshly grated orange peel in medium bowl; beat until smooth. Makes 1 cup glaze.

VANILLA GLAZE: Substitute 3 tablespoons water for orange juice and omit orange peel.

PIES

Chocolate Magic Mousse Pie

Makes 6 to 8 servings

1 envelope unflavored gelatin

2 tablespoons cold water

$1/4$ cup boiling water

1 cup sugar

$1/2$ cup HERSHEY'S Cocoa

2 cups (1 pint) cold whipping cream

2 teaspoons vanilla extract

1 packaged graham cracker crumb crust (6 ounces)

Refrigerated light whipped cream in pressurized can or frozen whipped topping, thawed

HERSHEY'S MINI KISSES BRAND Milk Chocolates

1. Sprinkle gelatin over cold water in small bowl; let stand 2 minutes to soften. Add boiling water; stir until gelatin is completely dissolved and mixture is clear. Cool slightly.

2. Mix sugar and cocoa in large bowl; add whipping cream and vanilla. Beat on medium speed, scraping bottom of bowl often, until mixture is stiff. Pour in gelatin mixture; beat until well blended.

3. Spoon into crust. Refrigerate about 3 hours. Garnish with whipped cream and chocolates. Cover; store leftover pie in refrigerator.

Easy Chocolate Cheesepie

Makes 6 to 8 servings

4 sections ($^1/_2$ ounce each) HERSHEY'S Unsweetened Chocolate Premium Baking Bar, broken into pieces

$^1/_4$ cup ($^1/_2$ stick) butter or margarine, softened

$^3/_4$ cup sugar

1 package (3 ounces) cream cheese, softened

1 teaspoon milk

2 cups frozen whipped topping, thawed

1 packaged crumb crust (6 ounces)

Additional whipped topping (optional)

1. Place chocolate in small microwave-safe bowl. Microwave at MEDIUM (50%) 1 to 1$^1/_2$ minutes or until chocolate is melted and smooth when stirred.

2. Beat butter, sugar, cream cheese and milk in medium bowl until well blended and smooth; fold in melted chocolate.

3. Fold in 2 cups whipped topping; spoon into crust. Cover; refrigerate until firm, about 3 hours. Garnish with additional whipped topping, if desired.

Chocolate Macaroon HEATH Pie

Makes 6 to 8 servings

$^1/_2$ cup (1 stick) butter or margarine, melted

3 cups MOUNDS Sweetened Coconut Flakes

2 tablespoons all-purpose flour

1$^1/_3$ cups (8-ounce package) HEATH Milk Chocolate Toffee Bits, divided

$^1/_2$ gallon chocolate ice cream, softened

1. Heat oven to 375°F.

2. Combine butter, coconut and flour in medium bowl. Press into 9-inch pie pan.

3. Bake 10 minutes or until edge is light golden brown. Cool completely.

4. Set aside $^1/_3$ cup toffee bits. Combine ice cream and remaining toffee bits. Spread into cooled crust. Sprinkle with $^1/_3$ cup reserved toffee. Freeze at least 5 hours. Remove from freezer about 10 minutes before serving.

Easy Chocolate Cheesepie

Chocolate Chip Cookie Dough Cheesepie

Makes 8 servings

COOKIE DOUGH
(recipe follows)

2 packages (3 ounces each)
cream cheese, softened

1/3 cup sugar

1/3 cup dairy sour cream

1 egg

1/2 teaspoon vanilla extract

1 packaged chocolate
crumb crust (6 ounces)

1. Prepare COOKIE DOUGH.

2. Heat oven to 350°F.

3. Beat cream cheese and sugar in small bowl on medium speed of mixer until smooth; blend in sour cream, egg and vanilla. Pour into crust. Drop COOKIE DOUGH by teaspoons evenly onto cream cheese mixture.

4. Bake 35 to 40 minutes or just until almost set in center. Cool completely on wire rack. Cover; refrigerate leftover pie.

COOKIE DOUGH

2 tablespoons butter or
margarine, softened

1/4 cup packed light brown
sugar

1/4 cup all-purpose flour

1 tablespoon water

1/4 teaspoon vanilla extract

1 cup HERSHEY'S SPECIAL
DARK Chocolate Chips or
HERSHEY'S Semi-Sweet
Chocolate Chips

Beat butter and brown sugar in small bowl until fluffy. Add flour, water and vanilla; beat until blended. Stir in chocolate chips.

Classic Chocolate Cream Pie

Makes 8 to 10 servings

5 sections ($^1/_2$ ounce each) HERSHEY'S Unsweetened Chocolate Premium Baking Bar, broken into pieces

3 cups milk, divided

$1^1/_3$ cups sugar

3 tablespoons all-purpose flour

3 tablespoons cornstarch

$^1/_2$ teaspoon salt

3 egg yolks

2 tablespoons butter or margarine

$1^1/_2$ teaspoons vanilla extract

1 baked (9-inch) pie crust, cooled, or 1 (9-inch) crumb crust

Sweetened whipped cream (optional)

1. Combine chocolate and 2 cups milk in medium saucepan; cook over medium heat, stirring constantly, just until mixture boils. Remove from heat and set aside.

2. Stir together sugar, flour, cornstarch and salt in medium bowl. Whisk remaining 1 cup milk into egg yolks in separate bowl; stir into sugar mixture. Gradually add to chocolate mixture. Cook over medium heat, whisking constantly, until mixture boils; boil and stir 1 minute. Remove from heat; stir in butter and vanilla.

3. Pour into prepared crust; press plastic wrap directly onto surface. Cool; refrigerate until well chilled. Top with whipped cream, if desired.

Mini Chocolate Pies

Makes 6 servings

1 **package (4-serving size) vanilla cook & serve pudding and pie filling mix***

1 **cup HERSHEY'S Mini Chips Semi-Sweet Chocolate**

1 **package (4 ounces) single serve graham cracker crusts (6 crusts)**

Whipped topping

Additional HERSHEY'S Mini Chips Semi-Sweet Chocolate or HERSHEY'S Semi-Sweet Chocolate Chips (optional)

Do not use instant pudding mix.

1. Prepare pudding and pie filling mix as directed on package; remove from heat. Immediately add 1 cup small chocolate chips; stir until melted. Cool 5 minutes, stirring occasionally.

2. Pour filling into crusts; press plastic wrap directly onto surface. Refrigerate several hours or until firm. Garnish with whipped topping and small chocolate chips.

Crispy Chocolate Ice Cream Mud Pie

Makes 8 servings

3/4 cup HERSHEY'S Syrup or HERSHEY'S WHOPPERS Chocolate Malt Syrup, divided

1/3 cup HERSHEY'S SPECIAL DARK Chocolate Chips or HERSHEY'S Semi-Sweet Chocolate Chips

2 cups crisp rice cereal

4 cups (1 quart) vanilla ice cream, divided

4 cups (1 quart) chocolate ice cream, divided

1. Butter 9-inch pie plate.

2. Place 1/2 cup chocolate syrup and chocolate chips in medium microwave-safe bowl. Microwave at MEDIUM (50%) 45 seconds or until hot; stir until smooth. Reserve 1/4 cup chocolate mixture; set aside. Add cereal to remaining chocolate mixture, stirring until well coated; cool slightly.

3. Press mixture, using back of spoon, evenly on bottom and up sides of prepared pie plate to form crust. Place in freezer 15 to 20 minutes or until crust is firm. Spread half of vanilla ice cream into crust; spoon chocolate sauce over layer. Spread half of chocolate ice cream over sauce.

4. Top with alternating scoops of vanilla and chocolate ice cream. Cover; return to freezer until serving time. Drizzle with remaining 1/4 cup chocolate syrup just before serving.

Chocolate Harvest Nut Pie

Makes 8 servings

¹/2 **cup packed light brown sugar**

¹/3 **cup HERSHEY'S Cocoa**

¹/4 **teaspoon salt**

1 **cup light corn syrup**

3 **eggs**

3 **tablespoons butter or margarine, melted**

1¹/2 **teaspoons vanilla extract**

¹/2 **cup coarsely chopped pecans**

¹/2 **cup coarsely chopped walnuts**

¹/4 **cup slivered almonds**

1 **unbaked (9-inch) pie crust**

Whipped topping (optional)

1. Heat oven to 350°F. Stir together brown sugar, cocoa and salt. Add corn syrup, eggs, butter and vanilla; stir until well blended. Stir in pecans, walnuts and almonds. Pour into unbaked pie crust. To prevent overbrowning of crust, cover edge of pie with foil.

2. Bake 30 minutes. Remove foil. Bake additional 25 to 30 minutes or until puffed across top. Remove from oven to wire rack. Cool completely.

3. Garnish with whipped topping and additional nuts, if desired. Cover; store leftover pie in refrigerator.

Creamy Milk Chocolate Pudding Pie

Makes 6 to 8 servings

1¹/₃ cups (8-ounce package) HERSHEY'S Mini Milk Chocolate Bars,* divided

²/₃ cup sugar

6 tablespoons cornstarch

2 tablespoons HERSHEY'S Cocoa

¹/₂ teaspoon salt

3 cups milk

4 egg yolks

2 tablespoons butter or margarine, softened

1 tablespoon vanilla extract

1 packaged chocolate crumb crust (6 ounces)

Sweetened whipped cream or whipped topping

*6 HERSHEY'S Milk Chocolate Bars (1.55 ounces each) may be substituted for the mini milk chocolate bars. Set aside 6 to 8 chocolate bar sections to use as garnish; proceed as above.

1. Set aside ¹/₄ cup small chocolate bars for garnish. Stir together sugar, cornstarch, cocoa and salt in 2-quart saucepan. Combine milk and egg yolks in bowl or container with pouring spout. Gradually blend milk mixture into sugar mixture.

2. Cook over medium heat, stirring constantly, until mixture comes to a boil. Boil and stir 1 minute. Remove from heat; stir in butter and vanilla. Add remaining chocolate bars; stir until bars are melted and mixture is well blended. Pour into crumb crust; press plastic wrap onto filling. Cool. Refrigerate several hours or until chilled and firm. Remove plastic wrap. Garnish with whipped cream and reserved small chocolate bars. Cover; refrigerate leftovers.

Easy Peanut Butter Chip Pie

Makes 6 to 8 servings

1 package (3 ounces) cream cheese, softened

1 teaspoon lemon juice

1²/₃ cups (10-ounce package) REESE'S Peanut Butter Chips, divided

²/₃ cup sweetened condensed milk (not evaporated milk)

1 cup (¹/₂ pint) cold whipping cream, divided

1 packaged chocolate or graham cracker crumb crust (6 ounces)

1 tablespoon powdered sugar

1 teaspoon vanilla extract

1. Beat cream cheese and lemon juice in medium bowl until fluffy, about 2 minutes; set aside.

2. Place 1 cup peanut butter chips and sweetened condensed milk in medium microwave-safe bowl. Microwave at MEDIUM (50%) 45 seconds; stir. If necessary, microwave an additional 15 seconds at a time, stirring after each heating, until chips are melted and mixture is smooth when stirred.

3. Add warm peanut butter mixture to cream cheese mixture. Beat on medium speed until blended, about 1 minute. Beat ¹/₂ cup whipping cream in small bowl until stiff; fold into peanut butter mixture. Pour into crust. Cover; refrigerate several hours or overnight until firm.

4. Just before serving, combine remaining ¹/₂ cup whipping cream, powdered sugar and vanilla in small bowl. Beat until stiff; spread over filling. Garnish with remaining peanut butter chips. Cover; refrigerate leftover pie.

Fudge Brownie Pie

Makes 6 to 8 servings

2 eggs

1 cup sugar

1/2 cup (1 stick) butter or
margarine, melted

1/2 cup all-purpose flour

1/3 cup HERSHEY'S Cocoa

1/4 teaspoon salt

1 teaspoon vanilla extract

1/2 cup chopped nuts
(optional)

Ice cream

HOT FUDGE SAUCE
(recipe follows)

1. Heat oven to 350°F. Lightly grease 8-inch pie plate.

2. Beat eggs in medium bowl; blend in sugar and melted butter. Stir together flour, cocoa and salt; add to butter mixture. Stir in vanilla and nuts, if desired. Pour into prepared pie plate.

3. Bake 25 to 30 minutes or until almost set. (Pie will not test done in center.) Cool; cut into wedges. Serve topped with scoop of ice cream and drizzled with HOT FUDGE SAUCE.

HOT FUDGE SAUCE

3/4 cup sugar

1/2 cup HERSHEY'S Cocoa

1/2 cup plus 2 tablespoons
(5-ounce can)
evaporated milk

1/3 cup light corn syrup

1/3 cup butter or margarine

1 teaspoon vanilla extract

Stir together sugar and cocoa in small saucepan; blend in evaporated milk and corn syrup. Cook over medium heat, stirring constantly, until mixture boils; boil and stir 1 minute. Remove from heat; stir in butter and vanilla. Serve warm.

Makes about 1 3/4 cups sauce

Chocolate Pecan Pie

Makes 8 servings

1 cup sugar

1/3 cup HERSHEY'S Cocoa

3 eggs, lightly beaten

3/4 cup light corn syrup

1 tablespoon butter or margarine, melted

1 teaspoon vanilla extract

1 cup pecan halves

1 unbaked (9-inch) pie crust

Whipped topping (optional)

1. Heat oven to 350°F.

2. Stir together sugar and cocoa in medium bowl. Add eggs, corn syrup, butter and vanilla; stir until well blended. Stir in pecans. Pour into unbaked pie crust.

3. Bake 60 minutes or until set. Remove to wire rack and cool completely. Garnish with whipped topping, if desired.

Peanut Butter and Milk Chocolate Chip Cookie Pie

Makes 8 to 10 servings

1/2 cup (1 stick) butter or margarine, softened

2 eggs, beaten

2 teaspoons vanilla extract

1 cup sugar

1/2 cup all-purpose flour

1 cup HERSHEY'S Milk Chocolate Chips

1 cup REESE'S Peanut Butter Chips

1 cup chopped pecans or walnuts

1 unbaked 9-inch pie crust

Sweetened whipped cream or ice cream (optional)

1. Heat oven to 350°F.

2. Beat butter in medium bowl; add eggs and vanilla. Stir together sugar and flour; add to butter mixture. Stir in milk chocolate chips, peanut butter chips and nuts; pour into unbaked pie crust.

3. Bake 50 to 55 minutes or until golden brown. Cool about 1 hour on wire rack; serve warm with sweetened whipped cream or ice cream, if desired.

Chocolate Pecan Pie

Chocolate Macadamia Truffle Mousse Pie

Makes 6 to 8 servings

1 cup HERSHEY'S SPECIAL DARK Chocolate Chips, divided

1/2 cup MAUNA LOA Macadamia Nut Baking Pieces, divided

3 tablespoons plus 1 cup (1/2 pint) cold whipping cream

1 prepared chocolate crumb crust (6 ounces) or 1 baked (9-inch) pie crust, cooled

1 teaspoon unflavored gelatin

1 tablespoon cold water

2 tablespoons boiling water

1/2 cup sugar

1/4 cup HERSHEY'S Cocoa

1 teaspoon vanilla extract

Sweetened whipped cream or whipped topping

1. Set aside 2 tablespoons chocolate chips and 1 tablespoon nut pieces. Place remaining chips, nuts and 3 tablespoons whipping cream in medium microwave-safe bowl. Microwave at MEDIUM (50%) 1 minute; stir. If necessary, microwave at MEDIUM an additional 15 seconds at a time, stirring after each heating, until chips are melted when stirred. Spread mixture on bottom of prepared crust. Refrigerate while preparing next steps.

2. Sprinkle gelatin over cold water; let stand 1 minute to soften. Add boiling water; stir until gelatin is completely dissolved and mixture is clear. Cool slightly, about 5 minutes.

3. Meanwhile, stir together sugar and cocoa in small mixing bowl; add remaining 1 cup whipping cream and vanilla. Beat on high speed of electric mixer, scraping bottom of bowl occasionally, until stiff. Pour in gelatin mixture, beating until just well blended.

4. Carefully spread over chocolate layer in crust. Cover; refrigerate several hours or until firm. Garnish with whipped cream and reserved chips and nuts.

Easy MINI KISSES Choco-Cherry Pie

Makes about 8 servings

1³/₄ **cups (10-ounce package)
HERSHEY'S MINI
KISSES BRAND Milk
Chocolates, divided**

1¹/₂ **cups miniature
marshmallows**

¹/₃ **cup milk**

1 **cup (¹/₂ pint) cold
whipping cream**

1 **baked (9-inch) pie crust,
cooled**

1 **can (21 ounces) cherry
pie filling, chilled**

Whipped topping

1. Place 1 cup chocolate pieces, marshmallows and milk in medium microwave-safe bowl. Microwave at MEDIUM (50%) 1¹/₂ to 2 minutes or until chocolate is softened and mixture is melted and smooth when stirred; cool completely.

2. Beat whipping cream in small bowl until stiff; fold into chocolate mixture. Spoon into prepared crust. Cover; refrigerate 4 hours or until firm.

3. Garnish top of pie with cherry pie filling, whipped topping and remaining chocolates just before serving. Refrigerate leftover pie.

NO-BAKE FAVORITES

Chocolate & Peanut Butter Truffles

Makes about 3^1/$_2$ dozen candies

^{3}/$_4$ **cup (1^1/$_2$ sticks) butter (no substitutes)**

1 **cup REESE'S Peanut Butter Chips**

^{1}/$_2$ **cup HERSHEY'S Cocoa**

1 **can (14 ounces) sweetened condensed milk (not evaporated milk)**

1 **tablespoon vanilla extract**

HERSHEY'S Cocoa or finely chopped nuts or graham cracker crumbs

1. Melt butter and peanut butter chips in saucepan over very low heat. Add cocoa; stir until smooth. Add sweetened condensed milk; stir constantly until mixture is thick and glossy, about 4 minutes. Remove from heat; stir in vanilla.

2. Refrigerate 2 hours or until firm enough to handle. Shape into 1-inch balls; roll in cocoa, nuts or graham cracker crumbs. Refrigerate until firm, about 1 hour. Store, covered, in refrigerator.

No-Bake Cherry Chocolate Shortcake
Makes about 6 servings

1 **frozen loaf pound cake (10^3/$_4$ ounces), thawed**

1 **can (21 ounces) cherry pie filling, chilled**

^{1}/$_3$ **cup HERSHEY'S Cocoa or HERSHEY'S SPECIAL DARK Cocoa**

^{1}/$_2$ **cup powdered sugar**

1 **tub (8 ounces) frozen non-dairy whipped topping, thawed (3 cups)**

1. Slice pound cake horizontally into three layers. Place bottom cake layer on serving plate; top with half the pie filling, using mostly cherries. Repeat with middle cake layer and remaining pie filling; place rounded layer on top. Cover; refrigerate several hours.

2. Sift cocoa and powdered sugar onto whipped topping; stir until mixture is blended and smooth. Immediately spread over top and sides of cake, covering completely. Refrigerate leftover shortcake.

120

Foolproof Dark Chocolate Fudge
Makes about 5 dozen pieces or 2 pounds fudge

3 **cups (1^1/$_2$ packages, 12 ounces each) HERSHEY'S SPECIAL DARK Chocolate Chips or HERSHEY'S Semi-Sweet Chocolate Chips**

1 **can (14 ounces) sweetened condensed milk (not evaporated milk)**

Dash salt

1 **cup chopped walnuts**

1^1/$_2$ **teaspoons vanilla extract**

1. Line 8- or 9-inch square pan with foil, extending foil over edges of pan.

2. Melt chocolate chips with sweetened condensed milk and salt in heavy saucepan over low heat. Remove from heat; stir in walnuts and vanilla. Spread evenly in prepared pan.

3. Refrigerate 2 hours or until firm. Remove from pan; place on cutting board. Peel off foil; cut into squares. Store loosely covered at room temperature.

Note: For best results, do not double this recipe.

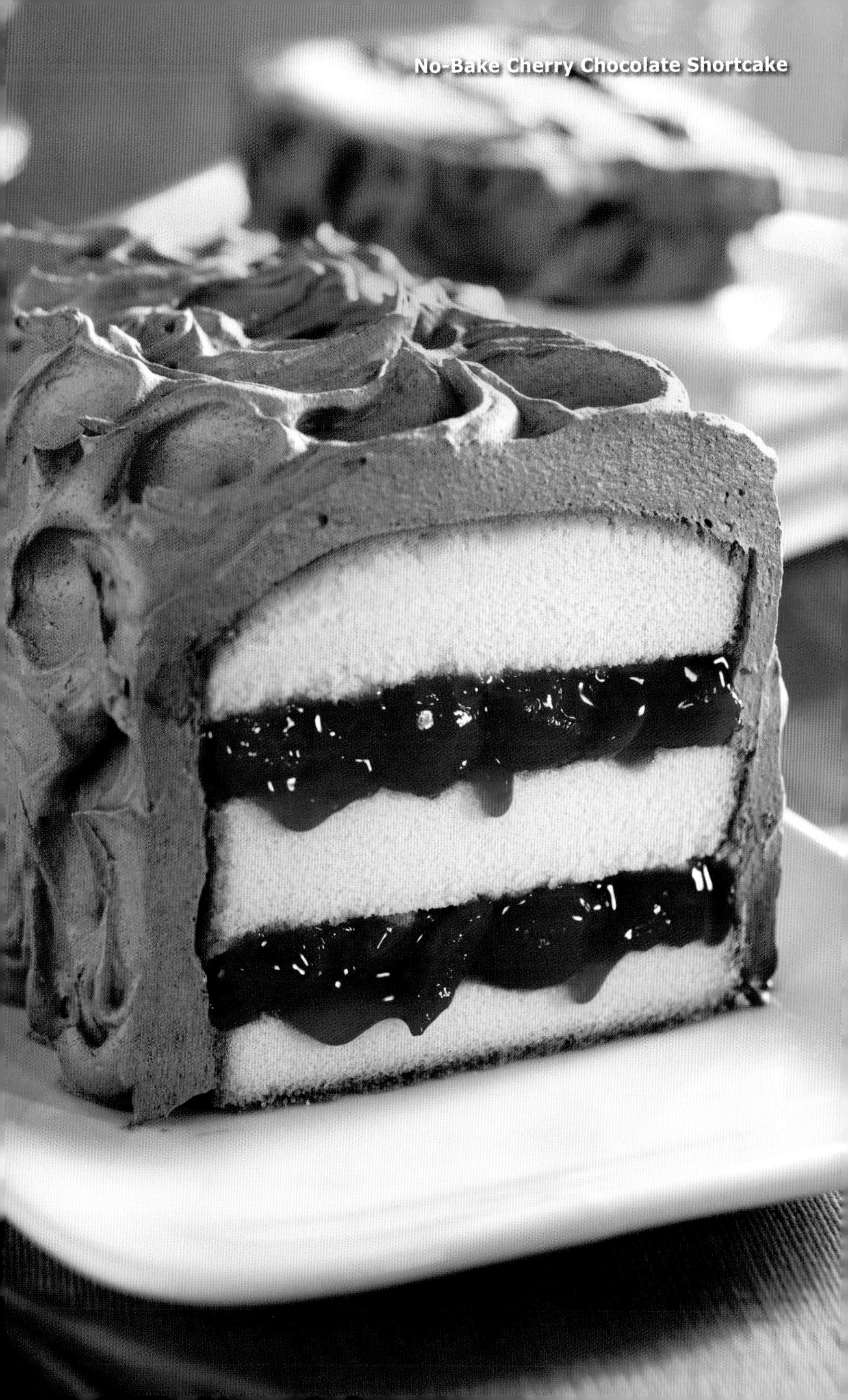
No-Bake Cherry Chocolate Shortcake

Easy Chocoberry Cream Dessert

Makes 10 to 12 servings

122

- 2 **packages (3 ounces each) ladyfingers, split**
- 1 **package (10 ounces) frozen strawberries in syrup, thawed and drained**
- 2 **envelopes unflavored gelatin**
- 2 **cups milk, divided**
- 1 **cup sugar**
- 1/3 **cup HERSHEY'S Cocoa or HERSHEY'S SPECIAL DARK Cocoa**
- 1/4 **cup (1/2 stick) butter or margarine**
- 1 **teaspoon vanilla extract**
- 2 **cups frozen non-dairy whipped topping, thawed**

  Additional whipped topping (optional)

  Fresh strawberries (optional)

  Mint leaves (optional)

1. Place ladyfingers, cut side in, on bottom and around sides of 9-inch springform pan.

2. Purée strawberries in food processor. Sprinkle gelatin over 1 cup milk in medium saucepan; let stand 2 minutes to soften. Add sugar, cocoa and butter. Cook over medium heat, stirring constantly, until mixture is hot and gelatin is completely dissolved. Remove from heat; stir in remaining 1 cup milk, vanilla and puréed strawberries. Refrigerate until mixture begins to thicken.

3. Fold 2 cups whipped topping into gelatin mixture. Pour mixture into prepared pan. Cover; refrigerate until mixture is firm. Just before serving, remove side of pan. Garnish with additional whipped topping, fresh strawberries and mint, if desired. Cover; refrigerate leftover dessert.

HERSHEY'S Premier White Chips Almond Fudge

Makes about 3 dozen pieces or 1^1/$_2$ pounds fudge

2 cups (12-ounce package) HERSHEY'S Premier White Chips

^{2}/$_3$ **cup sweetened condensed milk (not evaporated milk)**

1^1/$_2$ **cups coarsely chopped slivered almonds, toasted***

^{1}/$_2$ **teaspoon vanilla extract**

***To toast almonds:** Spread almonds in even layer on cookie sheet. Bake at 350°F 8 to 10 minutes or until lightly browned, stirring occasionally; cool.*

1. Line 8-inch square pan with foil, extending foil over edges of pan.

2. Melt white chips with sweetened condensed milk in medium saucepan over very low heat, stirring constantly until mixture is smooth. Remove from heat. Stir in almonds and vanilla. Spread in prepared pan.

3. Cover; refrigerate 2 hours or until firm. Use foil to lift fudge out of pan; peel off foil. Cut fudge into squares.

Note: For best results, do not double this recipe.

124

Chocolate-Orange Ice

Makes 6 servings

2 cups water

^{2}/$_3$ **cup sugar**

2 tablespoons HERSHEY'S Cocoa

Strips of peel from 1 orange

^{1}/$_2$ **cup fresh orange juice**

1. Stir together water, sugar, cocoa and orange peel in medium saucepan. Cook over medium heat, stirring constantly, until mixture comes to a boil. Reduce heat; simmer 5 minutes, without stirring. Strain to remove orange peel; discard. Cover; refrigerate mixture several hours until cold.

2. Stir orange juice into chocolate mixture. Pour into 1-quart ice cream freezer container. Freeze according to manufacturer's directions.

**HERSHEY'S Premier White Chips
Almond Fudge**

Lighter Than Air Chocolate Delight
Makes 8 servings

2 **envelopes unflavored gelatin**

$^1/_2$ **cup cold water**

1 **cup boiling water**

1$^1/_3$ **cups nonfat dry milk powder**

$^1/_3$ **cup HERSHEY'S Cocoa or HERSHEY'S SPECIAL DARK Cocoa**

1 **tablespoon vanilla extract**

Dash salt

Granulated sugar substitute to equal 14 teaspoons sugar

8 **large ice cubes**

1. Sprinkle gelatin over cold water in blender container; let stand 4 minutes to soften. Gently stir with rubber spatula, scraping gelatin particles off sides; add boiling water to gelatin mixture. Cover; blend until gelatin dissolves. Add milk powder, cocoa, vanilla and salt; blend on medium speed until well mixed. Add sugar substitute and ice cubes; blend on high speed until ice is crushed and mixture is smooth and fluffy.

2. Immediately pour into 4-cup mold. Cover; refrigerate until firm. Unmold onto serving plate.

Note: Eight individual dessert dishes may be used in place of 4-cup mold, if desired.

Refreshing Cocoa-Fruit Sherbet

Makes 8 servings

1 **ripe medium banana**

1 1/2 **cups orange juice**

1 **cup (1/2 pint) half-and-half**

1/2 **cup sugar**

1/4 **cup HERSHEY'S Cocoa**

1. Slice banana into blender container. Add orange juice; cover and blend until smooth. Add remaining ingredients; cover and blend well. Pour into 8- or 9-inch square pan. Cover; freeze until hard around edges.

2. Spoon partially frozen mixture into blender container. Cover; blend until smooth but not melted. Pour into 1-quart mold. Cover; freeze until firm. Unmold onto cold plate and slice. Garnish as desired.

Variation: Add 2 teaspoons orange-flavored liqueur with orange juice.

Creamy Chocolate and Peach Layered Pudding

Makes 6 servings

1/3 **cup sugar**

1/4 **cup HERSHEY'S Cocoa**

3 **tablespoons cornstarch**

2 2/3 **cups lowfat 2% milk**

1 **teaspoon vanilla extract**

PEACH SAUCE (recipe follows)

1/3 **cup frozen light non-dairy whipped topping, thawed**

1. Stir together sugar, cocoa and cornstarch in medium saucepan; gradually stir in milk. Cook over medium heat, stirring constantly, until mixture comes to a boil; boil 1 minute. Remove from heat; stir in vanilla. Press plastic wrap directly onto surface. Cool completely.

2. Meanwhile, prepare PEACH SAUCE.

3. Layer chocolate mixture and PEACH SAUCE in 6 individual dessert dishes. Cover; refrigerate until cold. Serve with dollop of whipped topping. Garnish as desired.

PEACH SAUCE:
Place 1 1/2 cups fresh peach slices and 1 tablespoon sugar in blender container. Cover; blend until smooth. Stir together 1/4 cup water and 1 1/2 teaspoons cornstarch in medium microwave-safe bowl until smooth. Add peach mixture; stir. Microwave at HIGH (100%) 2 1/2 to 3 minutes or until mixture boils, stirring after each minute. Cool completely. Makes about 1 1/3 cups sauce.

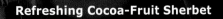

Chocolate-Covered Banana Pops

Makes 9 pops

3 **ripe large bananas**

9 **wooden popsicle sticks**

2 **cups (12-ounce package) HERSHEY'S SPECIAL DARK Chocolate Chips or HERSHEY'S Semi-Sweet Chocolate Chips**

2 **tablespoons shortening (do not use butter, margarine, spread or oil)**

1½ **cups coarsely chopped unsalted, roasted peanuts**

1. Peel bananas; cut each into thirds. Insert a wooden stick into each banana piece; place on wax paper-covered tray. Cover; freeze until firm.

2. Place chocolate chips and shortening in medium microwave-safe bowl. Microwave at MEDIUM (50%) 1½ to 2 minutes or until chocolate is melted and mixture is smooth when stirred.

3. Remove bananas from freezer just before dipping. Dip each piece into warm chocolate, covering completely; allow excess to drip off. Immediately roll in peanuts. Cover; return to freezer. Serve frozen.

Variation: HERSHEY'S Milk Chocolate Chips or HERSHEY'S Mini Chips Semi-Sweet Chocolate may be substituted for HERSHEY'S Semi-Sweet Chocolate Chips.

130

Festive Fudge
Makes about 2 pounds

3 cups (1^1/$_2$ packages, 11.5 ounces each) HERSHEY'S Milk Chocolate Chips

1 can (14 ounces) sweetened condensed milk (not evaporated milk)

Dash salt

^{1}/$_2$ to 1 cup chopped nuts (optional)

1^1/$_2$ teaspoons vanilla extract

1. Line 8- or 9-inch square pan with wax paper.

2. Melt chocolate chips with sweetened condensed milk and salt in heavy saucepan over low heat. Remove from heat; stir in nuts, if desired, and vanilla. Spread evenly in prepared pan.

3. Refrigerate 2 hours or until firm. Turn fudge onto cutting board; peel off paper and cut into squares. Store covered in refrigerator.

Semi-Sweet Festive Fudge: Proceed as above; using 3 cups (1^1/$_2$ packages, 12 ounces each) HERSHEY'S SPECIAL DARK Chocolate Chips or HERSHEY'S Semi-Sweet Chocolate Chips.

Chocolate Peanut Butter Chip Glazed Fudge: Proceed as above; stir in ^{2}/$_3$ cup REESE'S Peanut Butter Chips in place of nuts. Melt 1 cup REESE'S Peanut Butter Chips with ^{1}/$_2$ cup whipping cream; stir until thick and smooth. Spread over fudge.

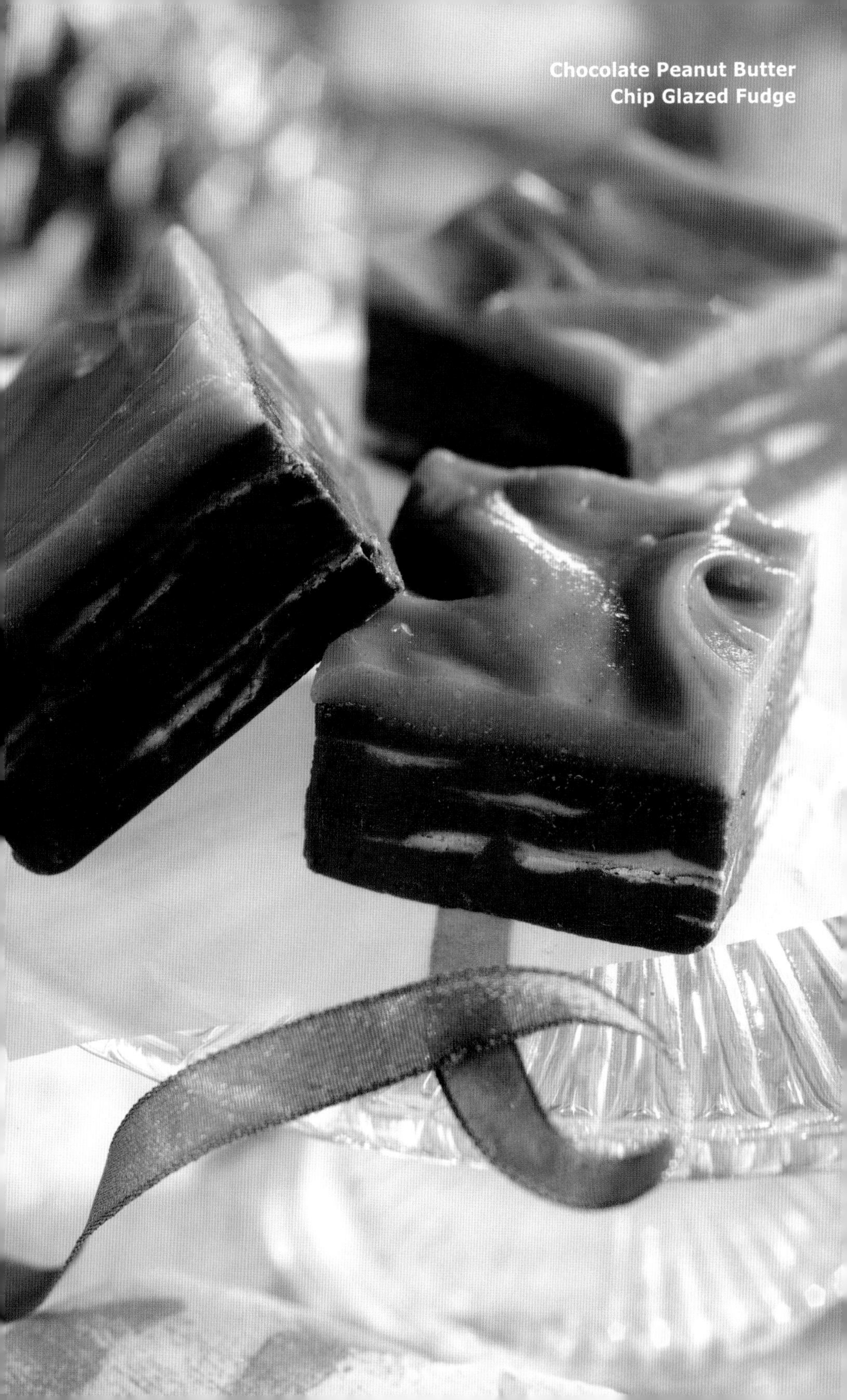
Chocolate Peanut Butter
Chip Glazed Fudge

Chocolate Buttercream Cherry Candies
Makes about 48 candies

134

About 48 maraschino
cherries with stems,
well drained

1/4 **cup (1/2 stick) butter,
softened**

2 **cups powdered sugar**

1/4 **cup HERSHEY'S Cocoa or
HERSHEY'S SPECIAL
DARK Cocoa**

1 **to 2 tablespoons milk,
divided**

1/2 **teaspoon vanilla extract**

1/4 **teaspoon almond extract**

**WHITE CHIP COATING
(recipe follows)**

**CHOCOLATE CHIP DRIZZLE
(recipe follows)**

1. Cover tray with wax paper.
Lightly press cherries between
layers of paper towels to remove
excess moisture.

2. Beat butter, powdered sugar,
cocoa and 1 tablespoon milk
in small bowl until well blended;
stir in vanilla and almond extract.
If necessary, add remaining
milk, 1 teaspoon at a time, until
mixture will hold together but is
not wet.

3. Mold scant teaspoon mixture
around each cherry, covering
completely; place on prepared
tray. Cover; refrigerate 3 hours
or until firm.

4. Prepare WHITE CHIP COATING.
Holding each cherry by stem,
dip into coating. Place on tray;
refrigerate until firm.

5. About 1 hour before serving,
prepare CHOCOLATE CHIP
DRIZZLE; with tines of fork
drizzle randomly over candies.
Refrigerate until drizzle is firm.
Store in refrigerator.

WHITE CHIP COATING: Place
2 cups (12-ounce package)
HERSHEY'S Premier White Chips
in small microwave-safe bowl;
drizzle with 2 tablespoons
vegetable oil. Microwave at
MEDIUM (50%) 1 minute; stir.
If necessary, microwave at
MEDIUM an additional 15 seconds
at a time, stirring after each
heating just until chips are melted
and mixture is smooth. If mixture
thickens while coating, microwave
at MEDIUM 15 seconds; stir until
smooth.

CHOCOLATE CHIP DRIZZLE: Place
1/4 cup HERSHEY'S SPECIAL DARK
Chocolate Chips or HERSHEY'S
Semi-Sweet Chocolate Chips and
1/4 teaspoon shortening (do not
use butter, margarine, spread or
oil) in another small microwave-
safe bowl. Microwave at MEDIUM
(50%) 30 seconds to 1 minute;
stir until chips are melted and
mixture is smooth.

White & Chocolate Covered Strawberries

Makes 2 to 3 dozen strawberries

2 cups (12-ounce package) HERSHEY'S Premier White Chips

2 tablespoons shortening (do not use butter, margarine, spread or oil), divided

1 cup HERSHEY'S SPECIAL DARK Chocolate Chips or HERSHEY'S Semi-Sweet Chocolate Chips

4 cups (2 pints) fresh strawberries, rinsed, patted dry and chilled

1. Cover tray with wax paper.

2. Place white chips and 1 tablespoon shortening in medium microwave-safe bowl. Microwave at MEDIUM (50%) 1 minute; stir until chips are melted and mixture is smooth. If necessary, microwave at MEDIUM an additional 15 seconds at a time, just until smooth when stirred.

3. Holding by top, dip $2/3$ of each strawberry into white chip mixture; shake gently to remove excess. Place on prepared tray; refrigerate until coating is firm, at least 30 minutes.

4. Repeat microwave procedure with chocolate chips and remaining shortening in clean microwave-safe bowl. Dip lower $1/3$ of each berry into chocolate mixture. Refrigerate until firm. Cover; refrigerate leftover strawberries.

Peanut Butter and Milk Chocolate Chip Cattails

Makes 12 to 14 coated pretzels

1 cup HERSHEY'S Milk Chocolate Chips, divided

1 cup REESE'S Peanut Butter Chips, divided

2 teaspoons shortening (do not use butter, margarine, spread or oil)

12 to 14 pretzel rods

1. Stir together milk chocolate chips and peanut butter chips. Place sheet of wax paper on tray or counter top. Finely chop 1 cup chip mixture in food processor or by hand; place on wax paper. Line tray or cookie sheet with wax paper.

2. Place remaining 1 cup chip mixture and shortening in narrow, deep microwave-safe bowl. Microwave at MEDIUM (50%) 1 minute; stir. If necessary, microwave additional 15 seconds at a time, stirring after each heating, until chips are melted and mixture is smooth when stirred.

3. Spoon chocolate-peanut butter mixture over about 3/4 of pretzel rod; gently shake off excess. Holding pretzel by uncoated end roll in chopped chips, pressing chips into chocolate. Place on prepared tray. Refrigerate 30 minutes or until set. Store coated pretzels in cool, dry place.

Variation: Melt entire package of chips with 4 teaspoons shortening and dip small pretzels into mixture.

Double Peanut Clusters
Makes about 2½ dozen clusters

1²/₃ **cups (10-ounce package) REESE'S Peanut Butter Chips**

1 **tablespoon shortening (do not use butter, margarine, spread or oil)**

2 **cups salted peanuts**

1. Line cookie sheet with wax paper.

2. Place peanut butter chips and shortening in large microwave-safe bowl. Microwave at MEDIUM (50%) 1½ minutes; stir until chips are melted and mixture is smooth. If necessary, microwave an additional 30 seconds until chips are melted when stirred. Stir in peanuts.

3. Drop by rounded teaspoons onto prepared cookie sheet. (Mixture may also be dropped into small paper candy cups.) Cool until set. Store in cool, dry place.

Butterscotch Nut Clusters: Follow above directions, substituting 1³/₄ cups (11-ounce package) HERSHEY'S Butterscotch Chips for Peanut Butter Chips.

Candy Cups
Makes 24 candies

2 **cups (12-ounce package) HERSHEY'S Premier White Chips**

1 **cup MAUNA LOA Macadamia Nut Baking Pieces**

1. Place white chips in medium microwave-safe bowl. Microwave at MEDIUM (50%) 1 minute; stir. If necessary, microwave at MEDIUM an additional 15 seconds at a time, stirring after each heating, until chips are melted and mixture is blended when stirred. Stir in nut pieces.

2. Drop by rounded teaspoons into small paper candy cups. (Mixture may also be dropped onto wax paper-lined cookie sheet.) Cool until set. Store in cool, dry place.

Variation: 1 cup coarsely chopped sweetened dried cranberries or dried apricots (or combination of the two) may be stirred into melted chip and nut mixture. Proceed as above. Makes about 36 candies.

Note: Recipe may be halved.

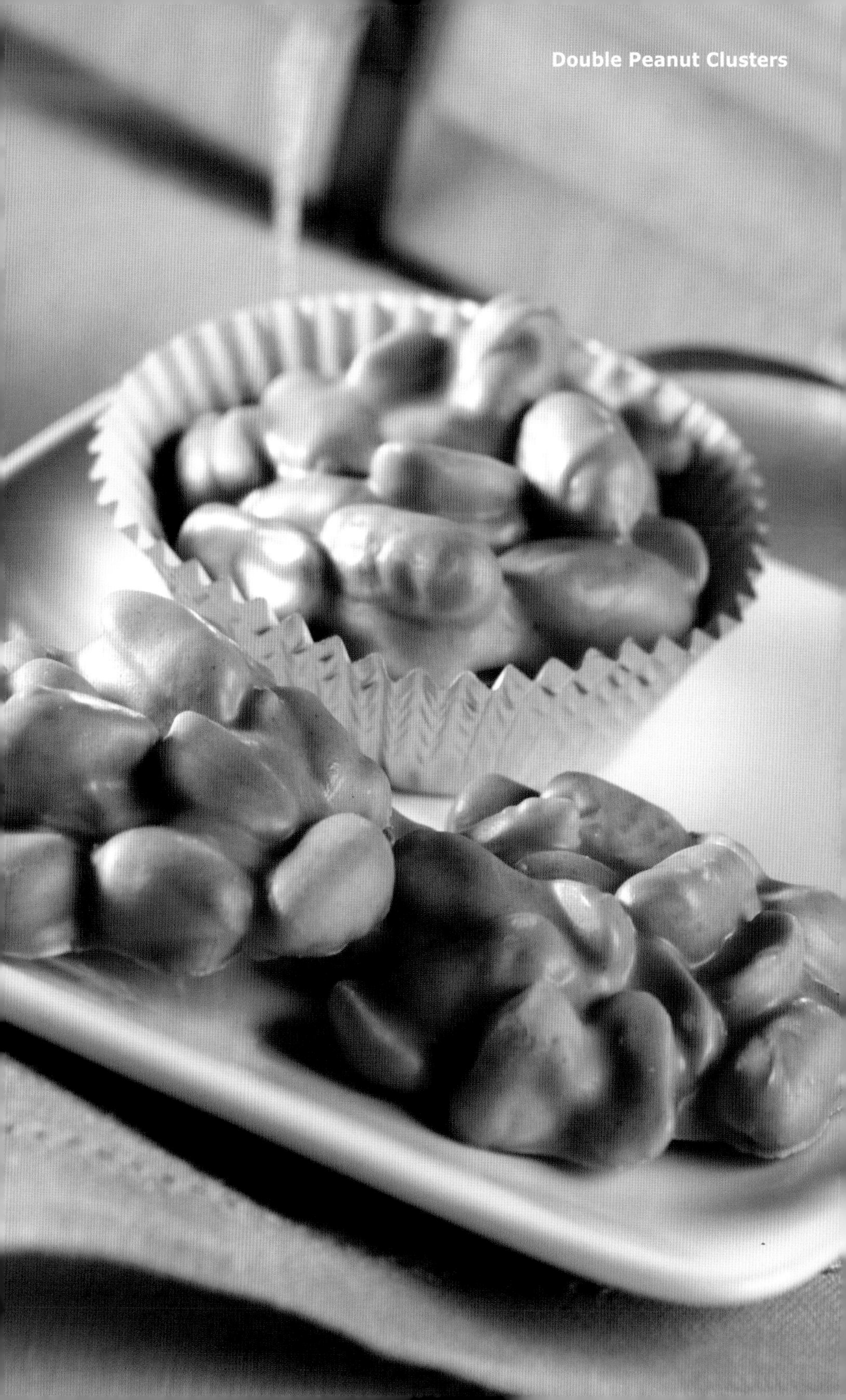
Double Peanut Clusters

KISSES Chocolate Mousse

Makes 4 servings

36 **HERSHEY'S KISSES** BRAND **Milk Chocolates**

1½ **cups miniature marshmallows or 15 regular marshmallows**

⅓ **cup milk**

2 **teaspoons kirsch (cherry brandy) or ¼ teaspoon almond extract**

6 **to 8 drops red food color (optional)**

1 **cup (½ pint) cold whipping cream**

Additional HERSHEY'S KISSES BRAND **Milk Chocolates (optional)**

1. Remove wrappers from chocolates. Combine marshmallows and milk in small saucepan. Cook over low heat, stirring constantly, until marshmallows are melted and mixture is smooth. Remove from heat.

2. Pour ⅓ cup marshmallow mixture into medium bowl; stir in brandy and food color, if desired. Set aside. To remaining marshmallow mixture, add 36 chocolates; return to low heat, stirring constantly until chocolate is melted. Remove from heat; cool to room temperature.

3. Beat whipping cream in small bowl until stiff. Fold 1 cup whipped cream into chocolate mixture. Gradually fold remaining whipped cream into reserved mixture. Fill 4 parfait glasses about ¾ full with chocolate mousse; spoon or pipe reserved marshmallow mixture on top. Refrigerate 3 to 4 hours or until set. Garnish with additional chocolates, if desired.

SPECIAL DARK Fudge Fondue

Makes 1¹/₂ cups

2 cups (12-ounce package) HERSHEY'S SPECIAL DARK Chocolate Chips

¹/₂ cup light cream

2 teaspoons vanilla extract

Assorted fondue dippers such as marshmallows, cherries, grapes, mandarin orange segments, pineapple chunks, strawberries, slices of other fresh fruits, small pieces of cake or small brownies

1. Place chocolate chips and light cream in medium microwave-safe bowl. Microwave at MEDIUM (50%) 1 minute or just until chips are melted and mixture is smooth when stirred. Stir in vanilla.

2. Pour into fondue pot or chafing dish; serve warm with fondue dippers. If mixture thickens, stir in additional light cream, 1 tablespoon at a time. Refrigerate leftover fondue.

Stovetop Directions: Combine chocolate chips and light cream in heavy medium saucepan. Cook over low heat, stirring constantly, until chips are melted and mixture is hot. Stir in vanilla and continue as in Step 2 above.

Deep Dark Mousse

Makes 4 to 6 servings

146

¹/₄ **cup sugar**

1 **teaspoon unflavored gelatin**

¹/₂ **cup milk**

1 **cup HERSHEY'S SPECIAL DARK Chocolate Chips**

2 **teaspoons vanilla extract**

1 **cup (¹/₂ pint) cold whipping cream**

Sweetened whipped cream (optional)

1. Stir together sugar and gelatin in small saucepan; stir in milk. Let stand 2 minutes to soften gelatin. Cook over medium heat, stirring constantly, until mixture just begins to boil.

2. Remove from heat. Immediately add chocolate chips; stir until melted. Stir in vanilla; cool to room temperature.

3. Beat whipping cream with electric mixer on high speed in large bowl until stiff peaks form. Add half of chocolate mixture and gently fold until nearly combined; add remaining chocolate mixture and fold just until blended. Spoon into serving dish or individual dishes. Refrigerate. Garnish with sweetened whipped cream, if desired, just before serving.

Milk Chocolate Pots de Crème

Makes 6 to 8 servings

2 cups (11.5-ounce package) HERSHEY'S Milk Chocolate Chips

1/2 cup light cream

1/2 teaspoon vanilla extract

Sweetened whipped cream (optional)

1. Place milk chocolate chips and light cream in medium microwave-safe bowl. Microwave at MEDIUM (50%) 1 minute or just until chips are melted and mixture is smooth when stirred. Stir in vanilla.

2. Pour into demitasse cups or very small dessert dishes. Cover; refrigerate until firm. Serve cold with sweetened whipped cream, if desired.

Chocolate & Fruit Snack Mix

Makes about 11 cups mix

1/2 cup (1 stick) butter or margarine

2 tablespoons sugar

1 tablespoon HERSHEY'S SPECIAL DARK Cocoa or HERSHEY'S Cocoa

1/2 teaspoon ground cinnamon

3 cups bite-size crisp rice squares cereal

3 cups bite-size crisp wheat squares cereal

2 cups toasted oat cereal rings

1 cup cashews

1 1/2 cups (6-ounce package) dried fruit bits

1 cup HERSHEY'S SPECIAL DARK Chocolate Chips or HERSHEY'S Semi-Sweet Chocolate Chips

1. Place butter in 4-quart microwave-safe bowl. Microwave at HIGH (100%) 30 seconds or until melted; stir in sugar, cocoa and cinnamon. Add cereals and cashews; stir until evenly coated.

2. Microwave at HIGH 3 minutes, stirring after each minute; stir in dried fruit. Microwave at HIGH 3 minutes, stirring after each minute. Cool completely; stir in chocolate chips. Store in tightly covered container in cool, dry place.

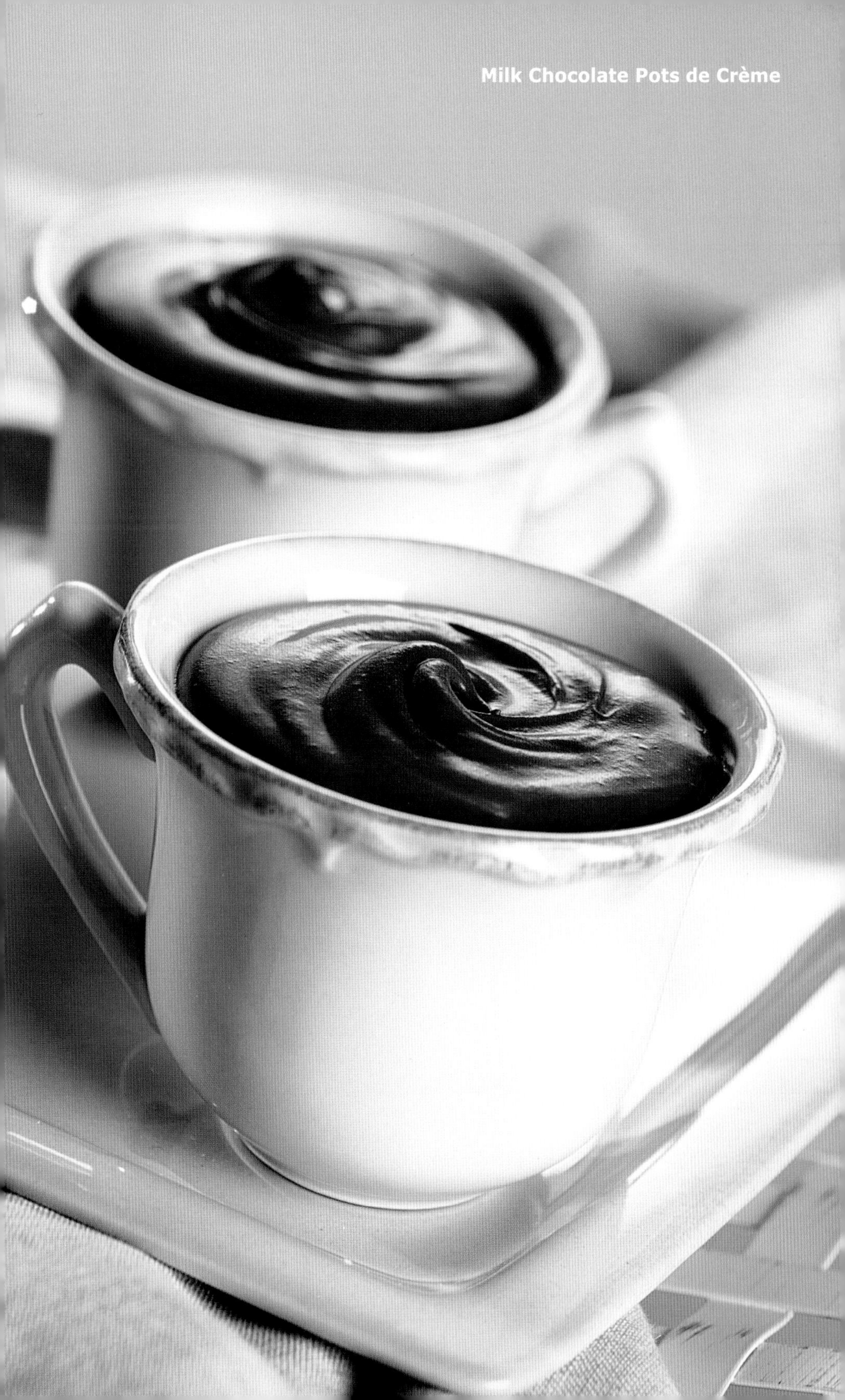

Milk Chocolate Pots de Crème

Butterscotch Nut Fudge

Makes about 5 dozen pieces or about 2¼ pounds fudge

1¾ **cups sugar**

1 **jar (7 ounces) marshmallow crème**

¾ **cup evaporated milk**

¼ **cup (½ stick) butter**

1¾ **cups (11-ounce package) HERSHEY'S Butterscotch Chips**

1 **cup chopped salted mixed nuts**

1 **teaspoon vanilla extract**

1. Line 8-inch square pan with foil, extending foil over edges of pan.

2. Combine sugar, marshmallow crème, evaporated milk and butter in heavy 3-quart saucepan. Cook over medium heat, stirring constantly, until mixture comes to full boil; boil and stir 5 minutes.

3. Remove from heat; gradually add butterscotch chips, stirring until chips are melted. Stir in nuts and vanilla. Pour into prepared pan; cool.

4. Refrigerate 2 to 3 hours. Remove from pan; place on cutting board. Peel off foil. Cut into squares. Store tightly covered in refrigerator.

HERSHEY'S SPECIAL DARK and Macadamia Toffee Crunch

Makes 1 pound candy

1 cup **HERSHEY'S SPECIAL DARK Chocolate Chips**

$1/2$ cup **MAUNA LOA Macadamia Nut Baking Pieces**

$3/4$ cup **(1$1/2$ sticks) butter**

$3/4$ cup **sugar**

3 tablespoons **light corn syrup**

1. Line 8- or 9-inch square or round pan with foil, extending foil over edges of pan; butter foil. Stir together chocolate chips and nuts. Reserve 2 tablespoons chocolate chip and nut mixture; sprinkle remaining chip mixture over bottom of prepared pan.

2. Combine butter, sugar and corn syrup in heavy medium saucepan; cook over low heat, stirring constantly, until butter is melted and sugar is dissolved. Increase heat to medium; cook, stirring constantly, until mixture boils. Cook and stir until mixture turns a medium caramel color (about 15 minutes).

3. Immediately pour mixture over chip and nut mixture in pan, spreading evenly. Sprinkle reserved chip mixture over surface. Cool. Refrigerate until chocolate is firm. Remove from pan; peel off foil. Break into pieces. Store tightly covered in cool, dry place.

White Chip and Macadamia Toffee Crunch: Substitute 1 cup HERSHEY'S Premier White Chips for HERSHEY'S SPECIAL DARK Chocolate Chips. Proceed as above.

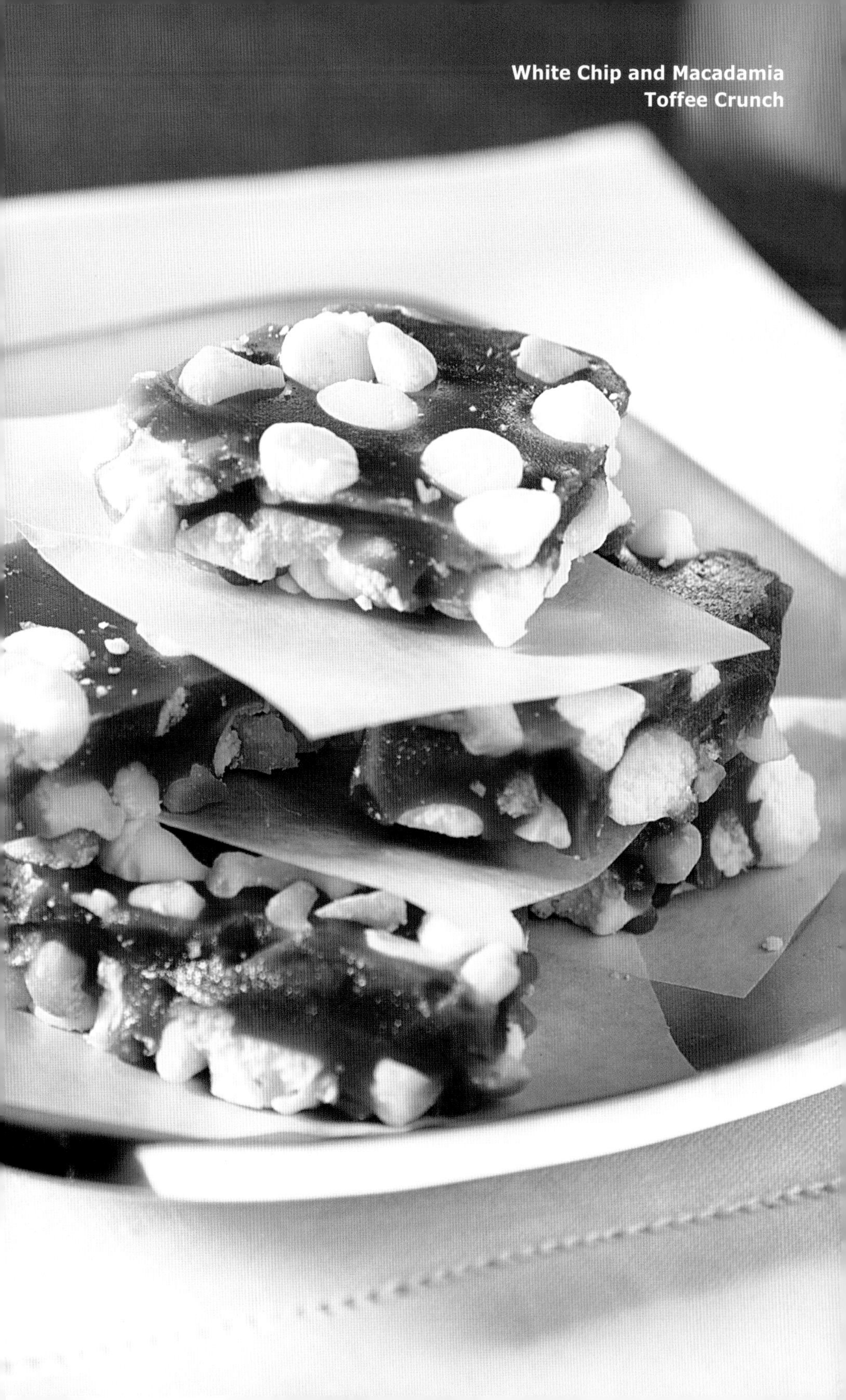

White Chip and Macadamia Toffee Crunch

Chocolate Lover's Ice Cream Sauce

Makes about 1 cup sauce

30 HERSHEY'S KISSES BRAND **Milk Chocolates**

1/2 cup HERSHEY'S Syrup

Any flavor ice cream

Sweetened whipped cream

Additional HERSHEY'S KISSES BRAND **Milk Chocolates (optional)**

1. Remove wrappers from chocolates.

2. Combine chocolates and syrup in small heavy saucepan. Stir constantly over very low heat until chocolates are melted and mixture is smooth when stirred; remove from heat.

3. Spoon sauce over scoops of ice cream. Garnish with sweetened whipped cream and additional chocolates, if desired. Serve immediately. Cover and refrigerate leftover sauce.

To reheat: Place smaller bowl containing sauce in large bowl containing about 1 inch very hot water. Allow to stand several minutes to soften; stir to desired consistency.

Microwave Directions: Combine chocolates and syrup in small microwave-safe bowl. Microwave on MEDIUM (50%) 15 seconds; stir well. Microwave an additional 30 seconds; stir until chocolates are melted and mixture is smooth when stirred. If necessary, microwave an additional 15 seconds or as needed to melt chocolates. To reheat refrigerated sauce, microwave on MEDIUM a few seconds at a time; stir. Repeat until warm.

INDEX

INDEX

157

METRIC CHART

VOLUME MEASUREMENTS (dry)

⅛ teaspoon = 0.5 mL
¼ teaspoon = 1 mL
½ teaspoon = 2 mL
¾ teaspoon = 4 mL
1 teaspoon = 5 mL
1 tablespoon = 15 mL
2 tablespoons = 30 mL
¼ cup = 60 mL
⅓ cup = 75 mL
½ cup = 125 mL
⅔ cup = 150 mL
¾ cup = 175 mL
1 cup = 250 mL
2 cups = 1 pint = 500 mL
3 cups = 750 mL
4 cups = 1 quart = 1 L

VOLUME MEASUREMENTS (fluid)

1 fluid ounce (2 tablespoons) = 30 mL
4 fluid ounces (½ cup) = 125 mL
8 fluid ounces (1 cup) = 250 mL
12 fluid ounces (1½ cups) = 375 mL
16 fluid ounces (2 cups) = 500 mL

WEIGHTS (mass)

½ ounce = 15 g
1 ounce = 30 g
3 ounces = 90 g
4 ounces = 120 g
8 ounces = 225 g
10 ounces = 285 g
12 ounces = 360 g
16 ounces = 1 pound = 450 g

DIMENSIONS

1/16 inch = 2 mm
⅛ inch = 3 mm
¼ inch = 6 mm
½ inch = 1.5 cm
¾ inch = 2 cm
1 inch = 2.5 cm

OVEN TEMPERATURES

250°F = 120°C
275°F = 140°C
300°F = 150°C
325°F = 160°C
350°F = 180°C
375°F = 190°C
400°F = 200°C
425°F = 220°C
450°F = 230°C

BAKING PAN SIZES

Utensil	Size in Inches/ Quarts	Metric Volume	Size in Centimeters
Baking or Cake Pan (square or rectangular)	8×8×2	2 L	20×20×5
	9×9×2	2.5 L	23×23×5
	12×8×2	3 L	30×20×5
	13×9×2	3.5 L	33×23×5
Loaf Pan	8×4×3	1.5 L	20×10×7
	9×5×3	2 L	23×13×7
Round Layer Cake Pan	8×1½	1.2 L	20×4
	9×1½	1.5 L	23×4
Pie Plate	8×1¼	750 mL	20×3
	9×1¼	1 L	23×3
Baking Dish or Casserole	1 quart	1 L	—
	1½ quart	1.5 L	—
	2 quart	2 L	—